We discussed the matter of making a work on California Wild Flowers, and made up our minds right then and there, that if the opportunity offered, to turn out for publication in colors and natural size, such a work as could be used by institutions of learning and might be appreciated by almost anyone, both from a scientific and artistic standpoint. In this I have tried to combine the two. While not a botanist, knowing absolutely nothing about botany, I have simply painted what I saw and how I saw it.—ALBERT VALENTIEN

Plant Portraits

the California Legacy

Margaret N. Dykens

Jean Stern

Exequiel Ezcurra

Peter Raven

with introductions by

Joan Irvine Smith

Michael W. Hager

of A.R. Valentien

THE IRVINE MUSEUM & SAN DIEGO NATURAL HISTORY MUSEUM

PLANT PORTRAITS:
THE CALIFORNIA LEGACY
OF A.R. VALENTIEN

Published on the occasion of
the exhibition *Plant Portraits:
The California Legacy of A.R. Valentien*
organized by the
San Diego Natural History Museum

Identification numbers used in the
catalogue refer to the inventory numbers
of the A.R. Valentien collection.

Full-page color plates are arranged in
alphabetic order of botanical names.

Unless otherwise noted, art is by
Albert Valentien and is in the collection of
the San Diego Natural History Museum.

©2003 The Irvine Museum
18881 Von Karman Avenue
Irvine, California 92612
949.476.0294 *phone*
www.irvinemuseum.org

All rights reserved. No part of the contents
of this book may be reproduced without the
written permission of the publisher.

LCCN 2003113133
ISBN 0-9714092-5-0 *cloth*
ISBN 0-9714092-6-9 *paper*

Edited by Jean Patterson
Designed by Lilli Colton
Type set in Perpetua with Fine Hand
Printed in Italy by I.G.E. Musumeci
through Overseas Printing

Front cover, page 6: ROMNEYA TRICHOCALYX
(Hairy Matilija Poppy, 9:46)
Back cover: OPUNTIA LITTORALIS
(Coast Prickly-Pear, 14:43)
Page 1: ROSA CALIFORNICA
(California Wild Rose, 11:15)
Page 2: QUERCUS KELLOGGII
(California Black Oak, 7:33)
Page 3: FOUQUIERIA SPLENDENS *(Ocotillo, 14:25)*
Page 8: HETEROMELES ARBUTIFOLIA
(Toyon, 11:29)
Page 11: DARLINGTONIA CALIFORNICA
(California Pitcher Plant, 10:26)
Left: NEMOPHILA MENZIESII VAR. ATOMARIA
(Baby Blue-Eyes, 17:20)

Contents

JOAN IRVINE SMITH	7	Foreword
MICHAEL W. HAGER	9	Introduction
	12	Plates I
MARGARET N. DYKENS	29	Albert Valentien's Flora of California
	57	Plates II
JEAN STERN	75	Albert R. Valentien and the Southern California Art Community
	93	Plates III
EXEQUIEL EZCURRA	113	A Wealth of Plants: The Ecological and Botanical Diversity of Southern California
	137	Plates IV
PETER RAVEN	153	The Importance of Global Biodiversity
	161	Plates V
	181	Appendix
	205	Index

Foreword

Joan Irvine Smith

The Irvine Museum is pleased to join the San Diego Natural History Museum in the publication of *Plant Portraits: The California Legacy of A. R. Valentien*. This unique collection of California's botanical biodiversity is an artistic treasure that has been hidden for too long. This beautiful book will at last make these wonderful paintings available to all of us.

Looking at these beautiful watercolors by Albert Valentien evokes childhood memories of how my mother, Athalie Richardson Irvine Clarke, took such pleasure in picnicking in the fields of poppies and lupines that covered hillsides at the time. I also recall how my grandfather, James Irvine, loved Matilija Poppies, and the stories he told of how he and my grandmother, Frances Anita Plum Irvine, would ride out on the Irvine Ranch to find these beautiful plants and carefully bring them back to place in their garden at the ranch house. If a road had to be widened on the ranch and an oak tree stood in the way, my grandfather would always reroute the road rather than remove the tree.

Conserving the environment and preserving the imperiled diversity of life on our planet are the two most important issues facing humankind today. Albert Valentien's work links fine art and natural history to bring public awareness to critical environmental issues. It is a timely reminder that these tasks need our immediate attention, not only on a global level, but also right here in our own state, county and community. If allowed to continue, the flagrant imbalance between the limited and diminishing resources of the land, water and air, and the increasing and unrestrained demands of humanity, will cause severe and irreversible consequences. The toll of these consequences will be paid in the extinction of numberless plant and animal species and will eventually threaten humankind itself.

The only way to achieve a balance between nature and humankind is for the environmental community to recognize the necessity of a strong and productive economic climate that will support environmental projects, and the development community, through its own enlightened self-interest, to pursue a positive environmental approach.

The splendor of nature fascinated Albert Valentien and inspired him to create these beautiful paintings. Today, with the renaissance of the glorification of nature in art, that spirit is motivating enlightened people in the same way it energized artists of nearly a hundred years ago. The common bond is the deep reverence for nature and the common goal is to preserve our environment, and no statement is more eloquent than the silent testament of these elegant paintings. Each generation, in its turn, is the steward of the land, water and air. Our time is now. I sincerely hope that the message this exhibition imparts will inspire us all to action in this most pressing obligation.

Joan Irvine Smith
President, The Irvine Museum

Introduction

Michael W. Hager

When I arrived at the San Diego Natural History Museum in 1991 and began to survey its collections, I was justifiably impressed by the 7.5 million specimens of minerals, fossils, plants, mammals, insects, and shells that had been carefully collected and cataloged by museum researchers since the institution's founding in 1874. Each drawer held a new natural treasure. I felt I couldn't be any more impressed until I went to the Research Library and discovered the trove of scientific books, periodicals, and antiquarian volumes that filled shelf after shelf, some works dating back to 1517. But the librarian had saved the best for last. Unlocking a cabinet and removing a large portfolio, her gloved hands reverently opened a folder and revealed a delicate watercolor painting. The botanical subject was so realistic that it seemed to float off the page. "These are the Valentiens," she said, and I was speechless.

Since then I've had the pleasure of giving countless museum tours, and I, too, leave the best for last, reliving my first Valentien encounter time and again as I watch visitors' initial reactions to this magnificent collection. As I observed my 10-year anniversary at the Museum, I was reminded of the decade that Albert Valentien devoted to the incredible task of recording California's botanical biodiversity in watercolor, and how this artistic legacy has inspired countless viewers since.

Certainly Valentien inspired his benefactor, Ellen Browning Scripps, who so treasured the paintings that she wouldn't donate them to the Museum until it had a fireproof building; Miss Scripps then provided the funds to construct that building in 1933. In the 1960s, the Valentiens moved the heart of another generous woman, Mary Clark, whose love of nature and eagerness to share this enthusiasm is now expressed in a spacious addition to the original building, the Mary and Dallas Clark Family Wing, which opened in 2001.

This book was made possible through the generous support of Joan Irvine Smith and James Irvine Swinden of The Irvine Museum of Irvine, Calif. In addition, Jean Stern, Executive Director of The Irvine Museum, who has had a long-standing appreciation for the work of Albert Valentien, has served as an encouraging and enthusiastic supporter of this project from the very beginning. The San Diego Natural History Museum is very grateful for the opportunity, as well as the expertise, provided by The Irvine Museum, enabling these hidden treasures of our large collection of hitherto unpublished Valentien paintings to be shared with the world at large.

Although the idea of this book had existed for many years, it would never have become reality without Eleanor and Jerome Navarra of San Diego, California, whose generous and far-sighted support has allowed the Museum to catalog, photograph, conserve, re-house, and protect the 1,094 Valentien paintings in its Research Library. Since October 1999, when Eleanor first viewed the paintings and she and Jerry decided to commit to this project, the Navarras have graciously and wholeheartedly supported much of the research and documentation necessary for the book. In addition, we are particularly grateful to them for their complete sponsorship of the exhibition, *Plant Portraits: The California Legacy of A.R. Valentien*, which premiered at the San Diego Natural History Museum in December 2003. This book is dedicated to them with heartfelt thanks.

Annette Winner, a long-time volunteer in the Botany Department and Research Library of the San Diego Natural History Museum, took it upon herself as a labor of love to examine every one of the 1,094 Valentien paintings, painstakingly updating nomenclature and conservation status, and compiling a comprehensive database containing all of the information gathered on each species. This book could never have been written without her selfless devotion to this project.

Philipp Rittermann photographed the entire collection of 1,094 paintings, installing a temporary studio in the Research Library for a period of several months. His unhurried, meticulous attention to quality and technical excellence, whether it involved testing of films or continuous comparison of the originals and the photographic copies, as well as his true appreciation of the artistic superiority of the paintings, convinced everyone involved that he was the only one for the job. He has also continued to assist us with photographic advice and support, and we are grateful that he was able to work with us on this project.

Bill Evans, whose flagship restaurant at The Lodge at Torrey Pines—A.R. Valentien—has been enormously successful since its recent opening, kindly provided us with the use of many historical photographs and documents from his personal collection of Valentien memorabilia.

Ruth Shelly, in her role as Deputy Director of Public Programs at SDNHM, played a very direct and personal role in shepherding this book from a concept to a reality. Ruth's patience, goodwill, and organizational skills were essential to the progress of the project.

We thank the Museum's Library Director, Margaret Dykens, for her tireless determination, not only to preserve the Valentien legacy, but also to advance appreciation and understanding of the collection. The Museum's Curator of Botany, Jon Rebman, provided invaluable technical advice, and Curatorial Assistant Judy Gibson researched and wrote captions for many of the illustrated species and provided other technical help.

Margaret Dykens, Exequiel Ezcurra, Peter Raven, and Jean Stern provided a context for the paintings reproduced herein with their essays and scholarship. The Museum's Exhibit Department provided design and installation of the handsome exhibition that accompanied this volume and toured across the United States.

Though he died without seeing his beloved watercolors published, I'd like to think that Albert Valentien would have been pleased with the joy and inspiration his paintings have provided for generations since.

Michael W. Hager, Ph.D.
Executive Director, San Diego Natural History Museum

Adenostoma fasciculatum
(Chamise, 11:20)
Chamise is most appealing when its branches are tipped with plumes of tiny white flowers. The heat of summer quickly dries these to a rusty brown, and the shrub takes on an aspect of toasted dryness. This resinous plant is often the dominant element in large swaths of chaparral—particularly on exposed southern slopes—and contributes greatly to the fire hazard in these areas.

Adiantum aleuticum
(Five-Finger Maidenhair Fern, 3:20)
This cold-climate Maidenhair fern is abundant on damp forest floors and cliffs in northern California, and ranges north to Alaska and across the Rocky Mountains. In this and other maidenhairs, the spore-bearing tissues are concealed beneath the rolled-under edges of the fan-shaped leaflets.

Aesculus californica
*(California Buckeye, 13:34)
The showy floral spikes of the
California Buckeye give way to
large green pods, which in turn
produce the shiny brown seeds—
sometimes called horse chestnuts—
that give the plant its name.
Though all parts are toxic, the nut
meal can be made edible by
leaching, and was a food used by
indigenous Californians. This
winter-deciduous small tree is
found in the mountains and
foothills of central California.*

ANEMOPSIS CALIFORNICA
(Yerba Mansa, 8:05)
This aromatic plant of streamsides and lake edges spreads via runners that root in the mud. Found in central and southern California as well as Baja California, it was used to treat diseases of the skin and blood and was well regarded by settlers—as indicated by its common name, Yerba Mansa, which means "gentle herb" in Spanish.

ASARUM CAUDATUM
*(Wild Ginger, 7:50)
The rhizomes of this low-growing plant with dark-green, heart-shaped leaves have a gingery, spicy odor. Wild Ginger prefers shady, moist areas where it spreads across the forest floor, and is easily overlooked even when in bloom, since the brownish-purple flowers are also at ground level. These strange blossoms have no petals— only three long sepals with tail-like ends. Indigenous peoples used Wild Ginger for teas and poultices.*

BALSAMORHIZA DELTOIDEA
(Balsam Root, 21:28)
Balsamorhiza, *or Balsam Root, is so-called because of the sticky sap found in the taproot of the plant. Found on sunny slopes with well-drained soils in northwestern California, Oregon, and British Columbia,* Balsamorhiza deltoidea *has showy blooms that appear in spring and summer. It is a member of the Asteraceae or Daisy family.*

Berberis nervosa
(Oregon Grape, 9:36)
This handsome shrub has glossy, dark-green leaflets and flowers in early summer. Native peoples ate the fruits and are reported to have made medicinal teas from the roots. It is found from British Columbia, Washington, and Oregon into central California, and was one of the plants collected in Oregon by the Lewis and Clark Expedition.

Bergerocactus emoryi
(Velvet Cactus, 14:46)
Thick stands of Velvet Cactus occur along steep ocean-facing hillsides where moist maritime fog encourages survival. From a distance, as the sun filters through the multitude of golden spines, a colony of these cacti takes on a deceptively smooth, velvety appearance. Found in southern San Diego County, on San Clemente and Santa Catalina islands, and throughout Baja California, the species is threatened by development, collection for horticultural uses, and feral goats.

CALOCHORTUS AMABILIS
(Diogenes' Lantern, 6:04)
Calochortus *flowers fall into one of two categories: nodding, or erect. This species, commonly called Diogenes' Lantern, falls into the nodding group. The delicate, deep yellow "lanterns" are commonly found in shady and open woodlands from the northern coast to central California.*

CALOCHORTUS SPLENDENS
*(Splendid Mariposa Lily, 6:07)
The delicate lilac or pink flowers
of the Splendid Mariposa are well-
named, as they present a splendid
show in early summer on hillsides
in chaparral and grasslands. This
plant prefers dry granitic soils and
occurs in Baja California north all
the way into the northern coast of
California. Native peoples once
dug the bulbs of* Calochortus *and
roasted them for eating, a fact that
attests to their relative abundance
in earlier times.*

CALOCHORTUS VENUSTUS
(Mariposa Lily, 6:17)
Valentien depicted beautifully the highly variable colors of this gorgeous species, which can range from white, yellow, pink, purple, to dark maroon, with many-colored blotches and stripes. The most important consistent characteristic is the presence of squarish spots on the petals, which are covered with hairs, as well as the recurved tips of the sepals. Wild populations of this plant in the Lily family, often found in grasslands and pinewoods, are threatened by loss of habitat and overzealous collectors.

Calochortus venustus
(Mariposa Lily, 6:23)

CALOCHORTUS VENUSTUS
(Mariposa Lily, 6:25)

CARDAMINE SP.
(Toothwort, 10:16)
This delicate annual in the Mustard family has pink blending to white flowers with four petals. The four petals of flowers in this family were once thought to resemble a cross and the family was therefore known as the Cruciferae, although now botanists refer to it more frequently as the Brassicaceae.

CARPENTERIA CALIFORNICA
(Tree-Anemone, 10:43)
The Tree-Anemone, with its showy clusters of large white flowers, is a threatened species of California. It is known from only seven occurrences in the foothills of the Sierra Nevada, and these are in areas threatened by development, logging, and grazing. In the same family as the better-known Mock Orange, it is also used as a landscaping plant. Unlike its relative, however, it keeps its dark glossy leaves year-round.

CEANOTHUS PROSTRATUS *(13:49)*
This creeping or "prostrate" species of Ceanothus, known as Mahala Mat, favors open areas in central and northern California coniferous forests where the deep-blue or purple flowers make a colorful carpet underfoot in April, May, and June. The name Mahala is believed to be derived from an Indian dialect for the word for woman.

CEANOTHUS TOMENTOSUS
(14:04)
This and other species of Ceanothus *are common in chaparral on hillsides and mountains throughout southern California. At the peak of their springtime bloom, the flowers can look like a purple mist over the hills. The name* tomentosus *refers to the fuzzy underside of the leaf.*

Albert Valentien's Flora of California

Margaret N. Dykens

The history of A.R. Valentien's paintings of the flora of California has all the elements one would normally expect in the story of a struggling artist's life—an abundant supply of natural talent, a longtime quest for beauty, a continuing battle for the financial means to further one's art, and the final heartbreak when life's closure comes before the goal can be reached.

Although he was to spend the last 17 years of his life in California, it is still fitting that Albert Robert Valentien was born in Cincinnati, Ohio, since that city is considered to be the birthplace of the Arts and Crafts movement in the United States. Albert was born on May 11, 1862 to Anna Marie (Wolter) and Frederick Valentine.[1] Albert showed artistic talent in his early years and started his training at age 13, attending the University of Cincinnati's School of Design, later called the Cincinnati Art Academy, working under Professor Thomas G. Noble. Noble was instrumental in securing a scholarship for the young artist.[2] Valentien worked at this school for five years, continuing his studies there under the tutelage of Frank Duveneck.[3]

When Valentien was 16, he and a fellow student named John Rettig became interested in the decoration of china, which was enjoying a new popularity. Valentien and Rettig began to experiment with the techniques of the time, and were affiliated with the Coultry and Wheately potteries in Cincinnati. According to Valentien's own notes, he first learned about underglazed pottery decoration from Thomas Wheately. Valentien and Rettig also taught classes in decorative art pottery-making locally, in the "Limoges style,"[4] which Valentien later described as the first class of its kind in the United States.[5]

In September 1881, Valentien was hired as the first regularly salaried employee of the decorating staff at the newly established Rookwood Pottery. He was only 19, but his career at Rookwood was to last for the next 24 years. Maria Longworth Storer, a wealthy Cincinnati woman who was much impressed with the artistry of Japanese decorative ceramics, had conceived of the company as a place where she could experiment freely with new ideas in pottery and particularly with underglazing decoration. From the very beginning, Rookwood was to be a place where artistic creativity was fostered and welcomed. William Watts Taylor, manager and president of Rookwood during the late 1880s and early 1900s, declared in later years that "whatever of artistic satisfaction lies in Rookwood is due first to the individuality of its artists, to their freedom of expression."[6]

Rookwood Pottery began in a somewhat amateur and tentative fashion, and like most such endeavors, progressed primarily through much trial and error. In looking back on his time at Rookwood, Valentien stated about the pottery and glazes for which Rookwood had become well known, "Such soft and delicate shades of pink, lavenders, yellows, and grays as are now being produced, were…then only things to be dreamed of…and many years of trials, discouragements, and failures passed by, before those effects became a possibility and later, a reality."[7] But Valentien and the other artists associated with Rookwood were not daunted by such challenges, and the name of Rookwood Pottery in time became famous for the quality of its unusual glazes, its outstanding decorators, and the high artistic value of its pieces.

Albert Valentien played no small part in that success. As he said later in his life, "I was the first regularly employed decorator—and served in the capacity of chief decorator for the period of 24 years during which time I originated and developed many of the chief effects which have made that institution famous throughout the world."[8] According to Kenneth Trapp, of the many artists employed at Rookwood over the years, the work of three decorators, namely Valentien, Matthew Daly, and William McDonald, "largely established Rookwood's reputation as the premier American art pottery."[9] At the height of his employment at Rookwood, Valentien supervised numbers of other decorators, while continuing to do his own pieces. He accomplished beautiful results and had a distinctive style of underglazed decoration with elegant fluency of line. Many of his pieces were acquired by such museums as the Victoria and Albert Museum in London, the Luxembourg in Paris, and the Royal Industrial Art Museum in Berlin.[10]

The decorators at Rookwood had a distinctive painterliness about their craft, and approached the vase in hand much as a painter would view a canvas, as a medium with which to showcase their art, rather than a mere ceramic vessel. The resemblance of the underglaze painting process in ceramics to techniques of oil painting has often been noted; the clear glaze applied over the decorator's painting gave a brilliance to the artwork on the pottery, much as the final varnish does to an oil painting.[11] An advertisement for Rookwood stated, "A vase made at Rookwood has the individuality of a fine painting. It is designed, decorated and signed by the artist just as a canvas is."[12]

Postcard of the Rookwood Pottery, Cincinnati, Ohio c. 1910, Private Collection

Albert Valentien, photograph courtesy of The Lodge at Torrey Pines

The company gained much in creativity because of its close association with the School of Design, and many of its employees had been trained as painters and artists at that institution. The school placed a heavy emphasis on drawing, with classes in drawing incorporated into all four years of classwork.[13] Thus, even if the decorators who came to Rookwood were new to ceramics, they had a good basic background in principles of art, drawing, or painting.[14] In addition, teachers at the school, such as Benn Pitman, offered classes that emphasized the use of local plants and flowers for decorative design, and required that students observe the various parts of plants, studying them in their natural habitat and sketching such details as roots, branching patterns, fruits and seeds, buds and blossoms. Therefore, many of the employees had already been trained in depicting forms from nature.

One of the other young decorators hired in the early years of Rookwood was Anna Marie Bookprinter, who was also a student of drawing and modeling at the Cincinnati Art Academy. Anna was born to Magdalene and Karl Buchdrucker, German immigrants who later anglicized their last name. Anna had worked for a year at the Matt Morgan Art Pottery, and then in October 1884 was hired at Rookwood, where she stayed for the next 21 years. Three years after starting to work together, Anna and Albert were married on June 1, 1887.[15]

Anna continued her studies at the Cincinnati Art Academy on a part-time basis while she worked at Rookwood. She was also a student of Frank Duveneck and studied sculpture under Louis T. Rebisso; in fact, sculpture was to become her true interest. In 1893 she exhibited a life-sized figure of Ariadne at the Chicago Exposition, and in 1894 won three prizes at the Art Academy for her work in sculpture. In 1895 she was awarded a gold medal for her life-sized sculpture "Hero Waiting for Leander" at the Atlanta Exposition.[16]

By the 1890s, Rookwood had grown from a fledgling enterprise into a successful, internationally known company, and had introduced its famous line of Sea Green

Anna Marie Valentien

Albert and Anna Marie Valentien, photograph courtesy of The Lodge at Torrey Pines

Left: *Vase, by Anna Marie Valentien, 1911–13, courtesy of Randy Sandler, photograph, Private Collection*

Right: *Rookwood pot (above) and Rookwood candle holder (below), courtesy of The Lodge at Torrey Pines*

and Iris ware. The Iris ware, true to its name, featured flowering plants as the subject of decoration far more than any other. Water lilies, orchids, milkweeds, poppies, dogwoods, roses, and wisteria were among the plants represented on these elegant ceramic pieces, often in pastels of soft pink, lavender, blue, gray, and green. According to Kenneth R. Trapp in Ellis' *Rookwood Pottery: The Glorious Gamble*, "By the early 1890s more than two hundred cultivated and wild plants were being painted at Rookwood. And this number continued to increase. Of course, other decorative subjects were painted, but none so dominated the decorative repertory as did blossoms and flora subjects."[17] Valentien and the other decorators studied plants from all available sources—from Rookwood's own gardens, from reproductions in books, from designs in textiles or other crafts. In some cases, flowers were even ordered specially so that the decorators could have fresh specimens to work from.[18] Rookwood decorators enjoyed Saturday field trips to study and sketch plants in their natural habitats.[19]

Valentien particularly liked the Iris line. He stated that it was one of his favorites, especially "when we were compelled to use flowers for decoration. In it I felt I could express all the quality of tenderness that the real flower contained, perhaps even more fully than on paper or canvas."[20]

The typical Rookwood piece at that time represented the plants in classic botanical illustration fashion, with no background detail such as other plants, earth, or sky. The plants were represented isolated from their milieu, and in this sense, resembled the aspect of natural history specimens. The flowers in particular were emphasized, and cultivated plants were featured more than native species, but the decorators paid close attention to botanical details such as tendrils or thorns, leaves, and stems.[21]

Rookwood supported the creativity of its decorators, bringing teachers in to train them, and sending employees to Europe to study different techniques, either from an artistic standpoint or to learn more details of the technology involved in mixing and firing glazes. Albert was sent to Europe for three months during the summer of 1894,

to study techniques of European pottery makers. Then in 1899, he traveled to Europe again to prepare the Rookwood Pottery exhibit for the Paris Exposition of 1900.[22] This was a particularly notable year for him because Rookwood received the Grand Prix in pottery and he won a gold medal for his personal contributions. In addition, one of his paintings of a winter scene in Cincinnati was accepted for exhibition at the Spring Salon. Anna had joined her husband in Europe after receiving a leave of absence from Rookwood so that she could study sculpture in Paris. She was a student at the Academy Colorossi and the Academy Rodin, where she took instruction from Auguste Rodin.[23]

It seems that Albert was not a particularly robust man, in terms of his physical health. For example, we know that he received an honorable discharge from service with the Ohio National Guard from December 1883 to February 1884, due to an unspecified illness,[24] and there were other periods in his life when he wrote of being unwell.[25][26] It was during a visit to the Black Forest in Germany in 1900, where Albert was recuperating from what he described as rheumatism,[27] that Anna suggested he try his hand at sketching the native wildflowers. This proved to be a turning point in his art career.

According to his own unpublished notes from about 1920, he "reasoned that there were very few flower painters and concluded to follow that branch of the Arts."[28] Perhaps the opportunity to manipulate and create the exact colors he wanted directly on the paper, as opposed to waiting for the intermediate steps of firing to see the results, was especially appealing to someone who had been painting flowers on ceramic ware. Whatever the reason, Albert became quite enamored with this new focus, and after returning to the United States in 1901, decided to become a flower painter, rather than continue with pottery decoration.[29]

Because they had heard about the beautiful flowers of California, the Valentiens decided to travel west. In 1903, they arrived in San Diego on the train to visit with

Rookwood vase, courtesy of Ray Redfern

Rookwood pot, Private Collection

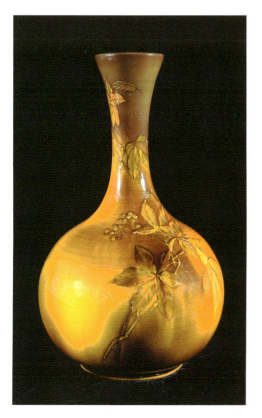

Pepper Tree, *watercolor with gouache, 24 x 19½ inches, courtesy of The Lodge at Torrey Pines*

Ellen Browning Scripps, c. 1923, photograph courtesy of the San Diego Society of Natural History

Anna's brother, Charles Bookprinter, at Honey Springs Ranch near Dulzura. According to Anna, they arrived on the train that was also carrying Carrie Nation, the famous abolitionist and member of the Women's Christian Temperance Union, although they were unaware of that fact until after they disembarked and saw the large crowd and brass band that had assembled. Albert teasingly remarked that his brother-in-law needn't have gone to so much trouble to welcome them to California![30]

Anna describes her impressions upon their arrival: "San Diego was a small country town at this time with no paved streets and few sidewalks. It was very dusty as there was a great shortage of water....Some beautiful old pepper trees impressed me very much....They were laden with pepper berries when first we saw them. I thought they were the most beautiful trees I had ever seen....[San Diego] seemed like a glimpse of paradise, no thunder, no lightning, with the most magnificent climate in the world; the hills and mountains were covered with wildflowers, especially the poppies. I shall never forget the joy and thrill we felt at the time. We knew we could not go back east to live, but must make our future home right here in San Diego."[31]

During his eight-month visit at Honey Springs Ranch, Albert painted 150 species of plants, which were then exhibited at the State Normal School in San Diego in September 1903. A clipping from the San Diego newspaper at that time describes the exhibit: "San Diegans were glad to greet such familiar friends as the manzanita, the California lilac, the matilija poppy, a favorite study of Mr. Valentien's. Perhaps the most admired study was of the pad cactus in flower, and as fiercely thorny as in life. As one small critic said, 'Look out! It will stick you!'"[32] This collection of paintings was purchased by an anonymous donor, who gave them to the Cincinnati Art Museum.[33]

Many visitors came to view this exhibit, probably including Ellen Browning Scripps.[34] Miss Scripps was a San Diego philanthropist and natural history devotee who had a great interest in the local plants and animals found in the diverse habitats of California. She was also a wealthy woman much interested in fostering education,

ARCTOSTAPHYLOS PUNGENS
(Manzanita, 16:14)

CEANOTHUS PALMERI
(13:47)

DICHELOSTEMMA CAPITATUM
(Blue Dicks or Wild Hyacinth, 5:47)
Blue Dicks are very common in grasslands, open woodlands, coastal sage scrub, and deserts. They are also known as Wild Hyacinth.

FRITILLARIA BIFLORA
(Chocolate Lily, 6:33)
Chocolate Lilies, with their nodding, satiny brown or greenish-brown flowers, are a sentimental favorite of many Californians, who remember seeing them in past years. Now they are uncommon, due in part to extensive development on the mesas and grassy slopes that they favor.

arts, and culture in her surrounding community. If she indeed enjoyed the exhibit, Miss Scripps would have undoubtedly been impressed with Valentien's skill at painting native California plants in an unusually vibrant manner. Five years later, the lives of Miss Scripps and Mr. Valentien would intersect once again.

After returning to Cincinnati, the Valentiens resumed their work at Rookwood, but the perfect climate, natural treasures, and lovely countryside of California had captured their hearts. In August 1905 they both resigned, ending their long association with the Pottery. Albert exhibited his flower paintings in Cincinnati, at the Pratt Institute in Brooklyn, New York, in Washington, D.C., and Chicago, and his work was met with critical acclaim. In 1908 they moved to San Diego, purchasing a home at 3905 Georgia Street for $4,500, where they were to live out the rest of their lives.[35] Miss Scripps conceived the idea of creating an artistic compendium of the flora of California, celebrating the diverse richness of native plants. In 1908 she commissioned Valentien to paint all the "wildflowers of California."[36] At the time, probably neither Scripps nor Valentien had any idea of the scope of the project in which they were getting involved.

California offers a highly unusual variety of climates and habitats, including coastal scrub, chaparral, low and high desert, salt marsh, oak woodlands, vernal pools, riparian, and many others. It is this diversity of habitat, joined with the state's geological and topographical variety, that results in such a wide diversity of flora. Botanists currently believe that the state of California includes more than 7,000 native vascular plant species,[37] of which about one-fourth are known as endemics,[38] meaning that they are species not found elsewhere. This species estimate is considered a conservative number, as there are new species being discovered every year. San Diego County alone is considered a "hot spot" of biological diversity and contains more threatened and endangered species of plants and animals than any other county in the continental United States. We are unaware of exactly how many species of plants in California

Above left: *Albert and Anna Marie Valentien, photograph courtesy of The Lodge at Torrey Pines*

Above right: *Albert and Anna Marie Valentien, c. 1910*

Below: *The Valentien home in San Diego*

were known to science at the time of Valentien's work, but botanical reports done by the California Geological Survey in the late 1800s included 3,450 vascular plant taxa.[39] Thus one can see the magnitude of the task that lay before Valentien.

Although neither Valentien nor Scripps were trained as botanists, they shared an acute interest in plants, and what expertise Valentien lacked in terms of botanical nomenclature and formal scientific education, he made up for by virtue of an uncanny eye for detail, including the smallest parts of a plant's flowers and fruits, and an untiring pursuit of specimens to paint, no matter how small or seemingly inconsequential the plant at hand. His work strived at all times for veracity in representation, never attempting to "prettify" a specimen. He also possessed an unerring accuracy in color. In addition, because of Rookwood, he already had many years of experience sketching and painting plants, albeit in a completely different medium.

Before he embarked on the project, he must have learned that a complete botanical illustration should represent the entire plant, including roots or bulb, stems, leaves, flowers, and fruits, if at all possible. In the instances when he was unable to represent the roots or bulbs of a plant, his notes state that it was because someone brought a less than complete specimen to him—for example, one that might have been cut off at the stem.[40] How much he studied other botanical artists' techniques we do not know, but the results of his painstaking work are accurate enough for botanists today to determine what species, and in some cases, even what subspecies he was illustrating—no small feat for an artist without any scientific training.

While Valentien's plant portraits are botanically accurate, they are unusual in the sense that they never appear to be stiff, artificial, or "pressed" on the page. On the contrary, his masterful depictions of such species as the poppies and cacti have a marvelous spontaneity and fluidity of line about them. Valentien must have had a very steady hand to be able to render such smoothly fluid stems and tendrils with never a hint of wavering brushstrokes. The paintings never look labored and even give the

CYPRIPEDIUM CALIFORNICUM
(California Lady's Slipper, 7:14)
Like many other species in the Orchid family, the California Lady's Slipper is threatened by logging and over-collecting. Because it has very specific requirements for germination, new plants are also very few and far between. It is found on moist slopes and along stream banks in central and northern California.

CALYPSO BULBOSA
(Fairy Slipper, top) and
SYNTHYRIS RENIFORMIS
(Snow Queen, bottom, 1:04)
The terrestrial orchid C. bulbosa is named after Calypso in Homer's Odyssey, *perhaps because of its beauty and mysterious nature. Like all orchids, it has a highly modified flower structure unlike that of any other plant family, featuring a slipper-like lip. The Fairy Slipper, as it is commonly called, has a single basal leaf and favors moist, shaded areas in coniferous forests. S. reniformis, which is unrelated to the orchids, has the charming common name Snow Queen and is found in grassy places in central and northern California up to Washington state.*

viewer a sense that the artist worked rather rapidly and freely, resulting in an extremely lively and vibrant representation. Valentien's early training as a pottery decorator undoubtedly played a role in this aspect of his later work. As noted by Kenneth Trapp in Ellis' *Rookwood Pottery: The Glorious Gamble*, "Underglaze painting demands concentration, patience, a steady hand and rapid execution. And yet the painted underglaze slip decoration must always appear entirely spontaneous."[41]

Between 1908 and 1918, Valentien traveled to many parts of this large state, collecting plants for his paintings. In an article in San Diego's *The Evening Tribune* for March 25, 1922, he is quoted as saying, "I have traveled over valleys, on mountain tops, along the sea shore, and in the deserts of the entire state, from Mexico to Oregon, looking for new specimens and painting them as I go."[42] Although we don't know many of the details of his travels, we know some facts from copies of his personal correspondence with his wife, with Ellen Browning Scripps, and with his friend, potter Albert Solon. For example, from the latter correspondence we learn that he spent several summers in Mendocino County, painting the local plants. In March 1912 he traveled to San Francisco, and later to Ukiah in Mendocino County, to paint flowers there.[43]

In March 1914 he wrote of his travels to Palm Springs in search of new plants to paint. In a letter to Ellen Browning Scripps (hereafter EBS) he describes arriving at the train station, six miles outside of Palm Springs, late at night with no one in sight to pick him up, so he spent the night as guest of a telegraph operator who "took pity" on him. He describes the many tuberculosis patients who were recovering in Palm Springs: "A dreadful and pitiful sight to see; nearly every one of them came to visit me and to see the [flower] studies and enjoyed them so much."[44]

In April, May, and June of 1914 he was in Cool in El Dorado County, painting a "yellow pine" on April 22, 1914, according to a letter to EBS. He also relates that he "hadn't been here but two days, when I contracted the most violent attack of oak poisoning that I have ever had, and for a day or two feared that I would have to go to

PAPAVER CALIFORNICUM
(Fire Poppy, 9:42)
The annual Fire Poppy, often found on burns, is named for its fire-following habits. It can also be found in places that have suffered other kinds of disturbances that allow the dormant seeds in the soil to germinate.

FRITILLARIA PLURIFLORA
(Adobe Lily, top) and
DODECATHEON HENDERSONII
(Mosquito Bills or Sailor Caps, bottom, 1:24)
The Adobe Lily is a rare plant of the foothills of central and northern California and southern Oregon. It is unusual in that it grows in very heavy, clay soils; hence, the common name, Adobe Lily. Beautiful lavender-purple flowers appear in February, March, and April on a single stalk. This lily is threatened by development, off-road vehicle traffic, grazing, and horticultural collection. Mosquito Bills, or Shooting Stars, are found in shady areas of northern and central California up to British Columbia and Idaho. The name Mosquito Bill probably refers to the fused stamens that extend from the center of the flower in a sharp point.

TOXICODENDRON
DIVERSILOBUM
(Western Poison Oak, 13:25)
The blazing autumn leaves of Poison Oak can lure the unwary Californian seeking holiday decorations to a miserable fate, as oils in its tissues cause allergic dermatitis in most people. Only at a distance can one safely appreciate the glossy beauty of this vine. It is not related to oaks at all; the name probably comes from the resemblance its leaflets bear to the shape of oak leaves.

DISTICHLIS SPICATA
(Saltgrass, 5:01)
Distichlis spicata, or Saltgrass, is a common, widespread species that grows on beaches, along estuary margins, and at the edges of desert palm oases; it is tolerant of salty and alkali conditions. This perennial grass has strong rhizomes and a distinctive, alternating herringbone leaf pattern. Salt grasses like this one have special glands to excrete excess salt, as well as other physiological adaptations to the extreme environment.

Frisco for treatment. My best eye was badly swollen, also my face, but they are now again in almost their normal condition, thank goodness."[45] Valentien's painting of poison oak gives silent witness to this ordeal. One wonders if he, being an Easterner, was unaware of the results of handling this toxic plant.

In the summer of 1914 he was in Tahoe and then at Cisco at 5,900-feet elevation in Placer County. In June 1914 he decided to expand his paintings to include the grasses, a particularly challenging subject for botanical illustration because of the extremely small and delicate nature of the reproductive parts of the plants. Despite the difficulty of representing relatively unshowy flowers and tiny structures, Valentien was to prove extremely skillful at depicting grasses; indeed, he says in one letter that some viewers describe them as his "best efforts yet". As he wrote to his patroness, "Everybody who sees them, thinks they are prettier than the flowers, and I think that you will like them also, at least, think them interesting enough to continue with them." We know he had completed his spectacular poppy illustrations by 1918, as he describes showing them in a letter to EBS dated that year.[46]

Of course, since his home was in San Diego, Valentien did much of his collecting and painting in the surrounding countryside. Years after his death, his wife described their collecting trips around San Diego County as some of the happiest times of her life: "Although the roads were not paved, they usually were kept in good condition. We had two covered boxes strapped to the running board. The larger of the two was covered with oilcloth. The other was tin and wicker. We took a number of newspapers along for packing the flowers. I have always loved flowers and this collecting of flowers will always be a joyous recollection. There were no restrictions on collecting flowers at that time, and we had them in greater abundance. It was a wonderful experience, this constant stumbling on new flowers you had never seen or even knew existed. It seemed to me that I could spot a new specimen no matter how fast the car would go."[47]

As he traveled throughout the state, Albert seemed to have a large network of friends, and friends of friends, who often provided him with a room that he could convert to a studio. As soon as he would arrive in a particular area, the word would go out among the neighbors that he was an artist who had come to paint plants in bloom, and many of the locals would supply him with fresh specimens. As Anna describes it, "Sometimes when we got up in the morning, we would find a bunch of wildflowers tied to the gate post."[48] Apparently, Albert was either not strong enough physically or did not enjoy going on many collecting trips himself; he seemed to rely on the assistance of local people to provide him with specimens.

Initially, it was an easy task to find new species to paint. But as the years went by, and Valentien had illustrated more and more of the commonly encountered plants, he had to range farther afield to pick up additional species. In 1914 he wrote from El Dorado County, "I am beautifully located and with a charming couple in a brand new house, away up in the mountains, and a thousand miles from nowhere…While there are lots and lots of flowers here, I find that I have already done the majority of them."[49]

One of Valentien's favorite subjects was the genus *Calochortus*, which displays its greatest diversity in California, with some 60 species and flower colors ranging from white to yellow to pink, purple, and bronze, with amazing variations in between. Because these beautiful members of the Lily family are eagerly collected, and because some occur in very few soil types or are threatened by development, many species are of special concern in terms of their conservation. One species was last collected in 1876 and is presumed extinct. Although Valentien by no means painted all of the species of *Calochortus* that we know occur in California, he depicted close to 30 species and seemed to relish the variety of detail—spots, hairs and color variations on nectaries on the petals—that distinguishes one species from another. Like many of the California flora that Valentien tried to capture in his work, this genus reflects the incredible richness and diversity of plant life that flourishes here.

POA FENDLERIANA SSP. LONGILIGULA
(Longtongue Mutton Grass, 5:06)
Longtongue Mutton Grass is a plant of mountain slopes.

MELICA IMPERFECTA
(Coast Range Melic, 5:13)
This native grass of dry, rocky hillsides and chaparral is found in the Sierra Nevada, Mojave Desert, southern coastal California, as well as Baja California.

Above left:
CALOCHORTUS VENUSTUS
(Mariposa Lily, 6:24)
Valentien especially enjoyed painting species of Calochortus, *a stunning genus in the Lily family that displays its greatest diversity in California, including 65 species that show a dazzling panoply of variation. The name* Calochortus *comes from the Greek for "beautiful grass"; the latter refers to the linear, grass-like leaves. Many of these species are of special conservation status, as they are either threatened or endangered plants and often have a very specific, restricted distribution.*

Above right:
CALOCHORTUS VENUSTUS
(Mariposa Lily, 6:17)

Below left:
CALOCHORTUS SPLENDENS
(Mariposa Lily, 6:08)

Below right:
CALOCHORTUS VESTAE
(Mariposa Lily, 6:11)
The bell-shaped flowers of C. vestae *range from white to purple in color, with blotches of red-brown surrounded by pale yellow. This plant prefers clay soils in pine forests or mixed evergreen woods.*

Above left:
CALOCHORTUS MACROCARPUS
(Mariposa Lily, 6:13)
The dramatic light-purple flowers of C. macrocarpus *are notable for their long, pointed sepals, which extend beyond the petals. Preferring volcanic soils, this species is a common sight in sage scrub and pine forests.*

Above right:
CALOCHORTUS VENUSTUS
(Mariposa Lily, 6:21)

Below left:
CALOCHORTUS VENUSTUS
(Mariposa Lily, 6:22)

Below right:
CALOCHORTUS VENUSTUS
(Mariposa Lily, 6:26)

Right: *Albert and Anna Marie Valentien at Torrey Pines*

Below left: *Albert Valentien painting outdoors, photograph courtesy of The Lodge at Torrey Pines*

Below right: *Albert Valentien working on flower studies, photograph courtesy of The Lodge at Torrey Pines*

By the time he had completed his work for EBS, almost 10 years after the project's inception, Valentien had illustrated some 1,500 species, including grasses, trees, and ferns in addition to the wildflowers he had originally contracted to illustrate. As he is quoted in an article in *The Evening Tribune* 25 March 1922, "The whole collection, if placed picture by picture, side by side, would reach more than a mile in length."[50] In hindsight, we can note species that he left unrepresented, but the sheer volume and consistently superior quality of his work remains awe-inspiring, particularly since it took place over such a long period of time.

The body of work that Valentien produced for the flora of California consists of 1,094 sheets of watercolor/gouache, on medium-weight pale gray wove paper 13 by 20 inches, mounted on linen backing, to form album pages. Valentien selected the paper primarily to serve as a foil for the white flowers he illustrated, which are considered by many to be his special forte. And it is true that such specimens as the boldly magnificent matilija poppy or the tiny, delicate inflorescence of the California sandwort, *Minuartia californica* (see page 111), are among the most arresting of his "flower portraits." He mounted the paintings on dressed linen to give them greater body and prevent tearing from handling.

Each specimen painted was later pressed and sent to Professor H.M. Hall at the University of California at Berkeley for identification.[51] Although it seems possible that herbarium specimens were made from these pressed and identified plants, unfortunately no such specimens have been located to date.

Despite the fact that there are 1,094 sheets, the number of species represented is closer to 1,500, because for many of the smaller plants, Valentien painted several specimens per page. Although there is occasional glazing of the dark colors, the majority appears to be watercolor alone. After completion, Valentien glued the paintings onto their linen backing, placed over each sheet a protective sheet of overlay and bound them into 22 volumes of ooze calf, each containing 50 sheets except for the

WOODWARDIA FIMBRIATA
(Giant Chain Fern, 3:29)
The Giant Chain Fern is easily identified, with fronds reaching as high as nine feet tall. Since it requires water year round, it is found only near streams, seeps, and springs. Indigenous peoples in California used it for thatching and basket weaving. Note the "chain" of sori, or spore sacs, shown on the underside of the leaflets.

POLYSTICHUM MUNITUM
(Western Sword Fern, 3:30)
The leaf-stems, or petioles, of Western Sword Fern are densely scaly, and the overall silhouette of the leaves could be described as sword-like. New leaves appear from the crown in spring as crosiers, or little curled fronds that later unfurl upward.

last volume, which had only 44. Each sheet was labeled with tags made of architect's linen in India ink in Valentien's own hand.

As Valentien completed his paintings, he delivered them to EBS, and the entire collection was kept in her home in La Jolla. In 1915, the collection was threatened when Miss Scripps' home suffered a devastating fire. Fortunately, Valentien's paintings had been stored in a separate fireproof outbuilding, so they were spared destruction.[52] Because of this near-tragedy, EBS later resolutely refused to donate the collection to any museum that could not demonstrate that the paintings could be kept in a fireproof space.[53]

Concurrent with their efforts on the flora project, Albert and Anna were also trying to establish a pottery in San Diego. It appears that although Albert was committed to the watercolor project, he could not completely abandon the call of his pottery skills, and also likely realized that the publication of the wildflower paintings was at best a distant goal. He and Anna faced a constant need to make ends meet financially. Undoubtedly, he believed that they could make extra money through a successful pottery operation. The San Diego area had good native clays; in 1886 a state mineralogist had discovered pegmatite and feldspar locally. Since these are necessary for the production of porcelain and pottery, this part of the country was viewed as a potential new center for the decorative pottery arts.[54]

We know a bit about the efforts to establish the Valentien Pottery in San Diego from the correspondence between Valentien and his friend and fellow-potter Albert Solon. Solon, who was Valentien's junior by 20 years or so, had moved to California at the same time as the Valentiens. By 1911, Solon was involved in helping the Valentiens set up a kiln in San Diego, as well as working at the California China Products Company in National City.[55]

Valentien gained financial backing for his new pottery from Joseph W. Sefton, Jr., a San Diego banker, and contracted with Irving Gill, the well-known San Diego

NEMOPHILA MACULATA *(Fivespot, lower right)*, TRIPHYSARIA ERIANTHA SSP. ROSEA *(Butter-and-Eggs, upper right)*, MIMULUS DOUGLASII *(Purple Mouse Ears, center left, 1:36)*
Valentien has masterfully depicted the miniature perfection of Nemophila maculata, *or Fivespot—notice the play of light on leaf and stem. This lovely white-flowered plant with purple spots on the tips of its corolla lobes is found in the Sierra Nevada and Sacramento Valley.* Triphysaria *grows on coastal fields and bluffs, whereas* Mimulus douglasii *prefers bare clay, granitic, or serpentine soils. Serpentine soils have unusually large amounts of iron and magnesium.*

Clockwise from top:
ERIOPHYLLUM WALLACEI
GLYPTOPLEURA MARGINATA
ERIOPHYLLUM PRINGLEI
SYNTRICHOPAPPUS FREMONTII
(2:08)
When Valentien painted plants that were very small, he often combined many species on the same sheet, as is the case here. These four diminutive plants are members of the Asteraceae, or Sunflower family, which is the largest family in California. All four plants are native species found in central and southern California.

architect, in 1910 to create plans for a pottery on Texas Street and University Avenue, with kiln, storage areas, and showroom.⁵⁶ Valentien needed other workers besides himself and Anna at the pottery, particularly since he was occupied at least part of the year with his flower paintings. In 1911 he hired Arthur Dovey, whom he had known at Rookwood.⁵⁷

Because the Valentiens' main skills were in decorating, they needed a person who could throw the pots correctly prior to decoration, as well as fire them. But Dovey's employment was to prove problematic for Valentien: apparently Dovey had a problem with carrying out his responsibilities. In 1912 Valentien wrote to Solon that he had "lost the kiln, and all the finest works I did, some 40 beautiful pieces were utterly ruined, besides the entire balance of the kiln, some 300 pieces or more. Then and there my ultimatum was given, and D. is only remaining long enough to finish turning up the balance of that famous Floral Association order.... We shall entirely reconstruct our affairs.... In the meantime, if you know anyone that can throw and turn, and fire, send him our way."⁵⁸

In 1912 Solon began teaching at Cathedral Oaks, an art school in Alma started by Frank Ingerson and George Dennison; he worked on tile-making and ceramics there. Valentien stopped at Alma to visit him on his way back to San Diego after flower painting up north. From his letters, it is clear that Valentien was hoping to enlist his friend's talents at the new pottery, if they could make it a financially viable enterprise. In July 1912 he writes that they have broken "ground for the new addition, the floor space of concrete to hold the machinery."⁵⁹

Due to various problems with the artistic side of his pottery, Valentien decided to concentrate on tile-making. In September 1912 he wrote to Solon to ask for assistance with a glaze formula for the tiles for "the Exposition," which was to be the Panama-California Exposition of 1915. Indeed, his financial backer in the pottery, J. W. Sefton, Jr., was serving on a committee planning for the upcoming Exposition. Some have

Valentien Pottery, San Diego

TETRACOCCUS DIOICUS
(Parry's Tetracoccus, 13:11)

LAVATERA ASSURGENTIFLORA
(Island Mallow, 14:08)

hypothesized that Sefton's interest may have been related to securing tiles for the Spanish Colonial buildings to be used in the Exposition.[60] Although there is speculation that Valentien created some of the tiles used in the dome of the California Building in Balboa Park, we have no proof of this.[61]

Valentien's letters, though resolutely optimistic, communicate his urgency for financial security. In his September 1912 letter he was still vague about when his pottery factory would be finished and when he would need Solon in San Diego. In June 1913 he wrote to Solon from Ukiah, where he was working on his flower studies, all about a trial firing of glazes that had failed. Indeed, the sad and continued failure of the Valentien pottery is summed up in a July 1913 letter to Solon written by Bruce Porter, an artist who worked at the Arequipa Pottery in Fairfax: "I journeyed out to the urban wastes and found Mr. Valentine (*sic*) in that hopeless state or environment that on sight takes the heart out of one. He seemed bravely pleasant with his failures all about him and spoke of a further trial of three weeks from his patron. I cannot believe that 3 weeks is miraculously going to right 3 years of successive disaster. One can't worry over him for his talents will find a market but the pottery product is as hopeless as any thing I ever saw."[62]

Finally, in September 1913, Valentien wrote to Solon, "More than $20,000 have already been expended on the pottery, and nothing to show for it, and I wouldn't blame anyone for not continuing with the concern under the existing conditions and unless better results were forthcoming."[63]

It is unclear exactly why the Valentien Pottery never succeeded. It is true that Valentien was only able to paint his plants during the flowering season of the year, which left him with other available periods of time to try to develop the pottery. But one is left with the lingering sense that he was, after the fashion of many other artists, hard-pressed to make ends meet financially, and ended up spreading himself too thin on his various projects, particularly when one takes into account the necessity of

traveling extensively for his plant studies. In a rare letter of less than optimistic tone to Solon from San Diego on September 25, 1913, he stated, "With the work at the pottery, my flower work, the mounting of them, and the pressed specimens, the condition of my eyes and the work at home—my daily life has been anything but a path of roses since my return and I hardly know at times where my head stands."[64] Although Anna tried to supervise the pottery in his absence, it is possible that, had Albert been in San Diego to manage the enterprise more effectively, their efforts to establish a pottery might have succeeded.

Meanwhile, Valentien persevered uncomplaining with his plant portraits. In 1922 there was an exhibit of the paintings at the Public Library, probably in La Jolla, which was seen by Charles Orcutt, a local amateur botanist and publisher affiliated with the San Diego Society of Natural History, who was also particularly interested in cacti and native plants of the area. In April 1922 he wrote to EBS and suggested that Valentien try to reconstruct the locality information for his paintings, as this would greatly increase their value for botanists, who are always interested in knowing where a particular plant was collected. In Orcutt's prescient words, "This collection, in later years as our wild flowers decrease or disappear, will be of very greatly increasing interest, and it seems a pity that the important data as to the exact locality where each flower was found, and the date when found in flower could not be preserved."[65]

Unfortunately, we do not have that information today. After Valentien's death, Anna, always hopeful that her husband's massive work would be published, wrote to EBS in September 1926, saying she had worked through all his notes and derived localities for all of the 1,094 sheets and was forwarding the list with locality data. As she states, "I am glad to help in any way possible—and will feel amply rewarded to see Mr. Valentien's work beautifully reproduced." But the whereabouts of this list remain unknown.[66]

In 1924, 16 years after he embarked on this ambitious project, Valentien made up

LILIUM PARRYI *(Lemon Lily, 6:40)*
The Lemon Lily is a rare plant that has nearly been extirpated from southern California. This beautiful lily, found near mountain streams in coniferous forests, is threatened by water diversion, grazing, and horticultural collection.

CALOCHORTUS PULCHELLUS *(Mount Diablo Fairy Lantern, top),* ERYTHRONIUM GRANDIFLORUM *(?) (Glacier Lily, bottom, 6:27)*
Under threat from urbanization and grazing, the Mount Diablo Fairy Lantern (top) is a rare plant. Named after Mount Diablo in Contra Costa County, this species is found only on wooded slopes and chaparral in the northeastern San Francisco Bay area. The Glacier Lily is found in subalpine meadows.

LANDSCAPE, *courtesy of*
The Lodge at Torrey Pines

a list of approximately 224 paintings that he deemed "most desirable for reproduction," in a letter to EBS.[67] From this letter it is clear that, since the completion of the project, he had scaled back considerably on his hopes for seeing even the majority of his 1,094 paintings published. We don't know when the decision was made, but apparently Miss Scripps had decided that publishing all or most of the paintings would be too expensive. According to some sources, Valentien had done the artwork at a very reasonable price with the hope that publication would finally cement his reputation as a painter; in some ways, he never recovered from his disappointment.[68]

From Valentien's correspondence and Miss Scripps' archives, we can deduce that, in the years immediately before Albert's death, the Valentiens, as well as employees of EBS, were making attempts to secure publication of at least a limited number of his paintings. In a letter from April 1925, only four months before Valentien's death, Miss Scripps' agent, J.C. Harper, wrote to an employee of the Scripps Newspapers in D.C., instructing him to go the Smithsonian to learn about the production of the series *North American Wild Flowers*. As he states, "For many years [EBS] has been having Mr. Valentien paint California wild flowers and there is a desire on the part of many botanists and flower lovers that some, at least, of these paintings of Mr. Valentien's shall be reproduced and published."[69] However, Mary Vaux Walcott, the wife of the fourth secretary of the Smithsonian, was to illustrate these volumes, so hopes for Valentien's work being published were once again dashed.

After the completion of Miss Scripps' contract, Valentien began to paint more landscapes in oil and explore other subjects. On August 5, 1925, at age 63, he died unexpectedly of a heart attack. The local papers carried an outpouring of sadness at his untimely death.[70]

It is doubtful that, at the inception of the California flora project, EBS had any idea how long it would take Valentien to complete it, or how expensive it would be to publish a book with so many full-color plates. Valentien can almost be seen as a

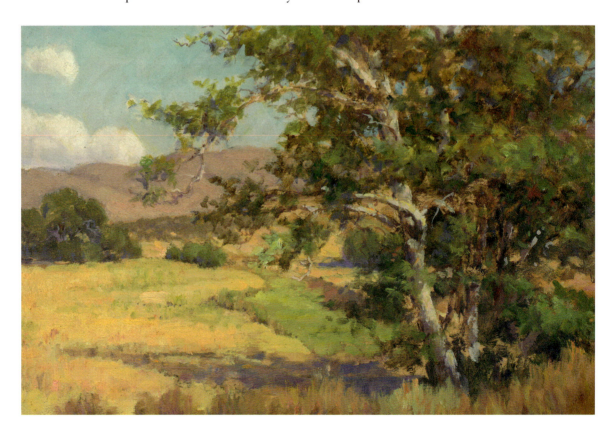

victim of his own proficiency; had he not been so prolific and so dedicated in his efforts, he might have produced only a few dozen flower masterpieces, which might well have been manageable for prompt publication. But because he endeavored to represent as many plants as he could, the body of work became so large that no suitable means was found to publish it before Miss Scripps' death.

Because EBS had served as Valentien's patron for so long, prospects for publication of his work died along with her in 1933. Until the present, only Miss Scripps and a few family members and friends were ever really aware of the sheer scope and dazzling proficiency of his effort. In comparison, Valentien's contemporary, the well-known bird illustrator Major Allan Brooks, who was commissioned by EBS to paint the birds of California, saw the publication of more than 100 of his full-color plates in 1923 in *The Birds of California* by W. Leon Dawson, to much critical acclaim. One can only hope that despite Valentien's lack of public appreciation and significant monetary reward, he gleaned a great deal of personal satisfaction from his work.

If Valentien ever had ill feelings towards EBS for not publishing his work, we have no evidence to that effect. However, he was said to have been very disappointed in the final outcome of all his efforts.[71] In a September 1917 letter to EBS he states, "Just what my Destiny will be and what work I will follow I am not at present prepared to say, but no matter what may be…I shall never forget the debt of gratitude that I owe you and the Scripps family in general."[72]

In March 1933, the entire collection of 1,094 paintings came to the San Diego Society of Natural History (the parent organization of the San Diego Natural History Museum (SDNHM)) through Robert P. Scripps, executor of Ellen Browning Scripps, after her death. Much later, in 1986, three larger Valentien flower portraits that had hung over the mantel in Miss Scripps' home also came to the SDNHM from Dr. Francis Smith, a physician and friend of EBS who had been loaned the paintings with the understanding that they were eventually to come to the museum after his death.[73]

The collection of paintings at SDNHM is unique in its scope. A set of 46 wildflower portraits by Valentien are kept in the California State Library in Sacramento[74] and a set of 50 similar paintings were said to have been purchased by Mrs. Frederick Remington.[75] In addition to the collection owned by the Cincinnati Art Museum, which consists of the early plant portraits that Valentien did when he first came west, these are the only known collections of significant size.

Although almost 100 years have passed since Valentien embarked on his flower portraits, with the touring exhibition of Valentien's flora of California, the public will at last be able to truly appreciate the exceptional scope of his efforts and witness the vibrancy, liveliness, and breathtaking abilities of this painter. Seen as a whole, his body of work gives us a tapestry that documents the spectacular richness of California's diverse plant life in the early 1900s.

Satureja douglasii
(Yerba Buena, 18:20)
This plant was named after David Douglas, a plant collector who covered over 1,000 miles in California from 1830 to 1832, investigating plants that could be brought back to England. He collected almost 500 species previously unknown to botany. For many of these, he shipped seeds back to Europe, where such plants as the California poppy, lupines, and irises were to become popular garden plants. Yerba Buena ("the good herb") has been used medicinally for almost every ailment, and dried leaves make a pleasant tea. It is a trailing plant that forms mats on shady woodland floors and in the chaparral.

Acknowledgements

Pamela Bury of Santa Barbara, Calif. generously shared primary sources with me; her own research into early pottery-making in California uncovered the relationship between her grandfather Albert Solon and Albert Valentien. Thank you, Pamela, for providing me with a treasure trove of copies of original correspondence between Solon and Valentien. Also, Judy Harvey-Sahak, librarian and archivist for the Ellen Browning Scripps papers at Denison Library, Scripps College in Claremont, Calif. gave of her time in searching out original correspondence between Ellen Browning Scripps and Albert Valentien as well as other correspondents in regard to the flora of California project.

Although I could not travel to Cincinnati to secure copies of the family memorabilia and correspondence gathered for the *Albert Valentien: The California Years* exhibit in 2000 at the Cincinnati Art Galleries, Randy Sandler and Tammy Williford spoke with me about it, generously made copies of numerous documents, and forwarded them to me at my request. In addition, Kristin Spangenberg, Curator of Prints, Drawings, and Photographs at the Cincinnati Art Museum, mailed me copies from her curatorial files of original notes made by Valentien. Judy Gibson and Dr. Jon Rebman of our Botany Department have provided much-appreciated expert advice and suggestions over the course of this research. Lastly, I would like to acknowledge the encouragement of Dale Clark and Exequiel Ezcurra, who have shared my almost evangelical interest in the Valentien collection and supported my efforts from the beginning.

Above left:
Pentagramma triangularis ssp. triangularis *(Goldback Fern or Silverback Fern, 3:16) The common name for ferns in the genus* Pentagramma *is Goldback or Silverback Fern. It is common in rock crevices or in dry soil in wooded areas. Observe how Valentien shows the play of light on the waxy powder found on the reverse side of this delicate fern's fronds.*

Above right: Dryopteris arguta *(Coastal Wood Fern, 3:33) This is a large plant when mature, with somewhat leathery, deep green leaves that are 12 to 30 inches long and twice-pinnate—meaning in the form of a feather, with leaflets arranged along each side of the central stalk. For the artist, depicting a fern can be tedious since there are so many repetitions of the tiny leaflets with their perfectly regular form; note the meticulous care of Valentien's rendering.*

Below left: Lamarckia aurea *(5:03)*

Below right: Ranunculus sp. *(Buttercup, 9:31)*

SILENE HOOKERI
(Hooker's Silene, 9:09)
A member of the Pink family, Silene hookeri *is found in open areas, slopes, and the coniferous and oak woods of northern California and Oregon.*

NOTES

1. According to Kenneth Trapp in *The Arts and Crafts Movement in California: Living the Good Life* (New York: Abbeville Press, 1993), Valentine changed the spelling of his name to Valentien between 1882–1883.
2. Albert R. Valentien, "Rookwood, or to be more concise, Rookwood Pottery," Unpublished, handwritten notes, undated, 15 pages.
3. Bruce Kamerling, "Anna and Albert Valentien: The Arts and Crafts Movement in San Diego," *Journal of San Diego History* 24:2 (Spring 1978).
4. Nancy E. Owen, *Rookwood and the Industry of Art: Women, Culture and Commerce, 1880–1913* (Athens, Ohio: Ohio University Press, 2001).
5. Valentien, "Rookwood, or to be more concise, Rookwood Pottery."
6. Owen, *Rookwood and the Industry of Art*, 52.
7. Valentien, "Rookwood, or to be more concise, Rookwood Pottery."
8. Albert R. Valentien, "Biographical notes of Albert R. Valentien," unpublished typescript from pencil notes, circa 1920, 3 unnumbered pages.
9. Kenneth R. Trapp, *Ode to Nature: Flowers and Landscapes of the Rookwood Pottery 1880–1940*, April 15–June 30, 1980 (New York: Jordan-Volpe Gallery, distributed by P. Smith, 1980) 20.
10. *Albert R. Valentien: The California Years, 1908–1925* (Cincinnati, Ohio: Cincinnati Art Galleries, 2000) 2.
11. Trapp, *Ode to Nature*.
12. Owen, *Rookwood and the Industry of Art*, 107.
13. Trapp, *Ode to Nature*.
14. Anita Ellis, *Rookwood Pottery: The Glorious Gamble* (Cincinnati, Ohio: Cincinnati Art Museum; New York: Rizzoli, 1992).
15. Kamerling, "Anna and Albert Valentien."
16. Ibid.
17. Ellis, *Rookwood Pottery: The Glorious Gamble*, 21.
18. Owen, *Rookwood and the Industry of Art*, 217.
19. Trapp, *Ode to Nature*.
20. Owen, *Rookwood and the Industry of Art*, 218.
21. Ellis, *Rookwood Pottery: The Glorious Gamble*.
22. Kamerling, "Anna and Albert Valentien."
23. Ibid.
24. From photocopy of original document.
25. Personal notes written by ARV, from Cincinnati Art Museum curatorial files.
26. Indeed, work in ceramics was known to involve health hazards at the time. For example, the high-gloss glazes such as those employed at Rookwood in the earlier years contained high amounts of lead. See Owen, *Rookwood and the Industry of Art*, 268. We have no way of knowing if Valentien's repeated exposures to hazardous chemicals may have affected his health, however.
27. Personal notes written by ARV, from Cincinnati Art Museum curatorial files.

28. Valentien, "Biographical notes of Albert R. Valentien," 1.

29. Personal notes written by ARV, from Cincinnati Art Museum curatorial files.

30. Anna Marie Bookprinter Valentien, unpublished handwritten notes.

31. Ibid.

32. *San Diego Union*, 19 September 1903.

33. Personal notes written by ARV, from Cincinnati Art Museum curatorial files.

34. Esther B. Hardisty, "Priceless Paintings in San Diego Museum of Natural History: The Life and Works of Albert R. Valentien," unpublished typescript, 7 unnumbered pages.

35. Kamerling, "Anna and Albert Valentien."

36. Valentien, "Biographical notes of Albert R. Valentien."

37. Barbara Ertter, "Floristic Surprises in North America North of Mexico," *Annals of the Missouri Botanical Garden* 87 (2000): 81–109.

38. James C. Hickman, ed., *The Jepson Manual: Higher Plants of California* (Berkeley: University of California Press, 1993).

39. Ertter, "Floristic Surprises in North America North of Mexico."

40. Personal notes written by ARV, from Cincinnati Art Museum curatorial files.

41. Ellis, *Rookwood Pottery: The Glorious Gamble*, 21.

42. *The Evening Tribune* (probably La Jolla, Calif.), 25 March 1922.

43. ARV to potter Albert Solon, original correspondence owned by Pamela Bury, Solon's granddaughter.

44. ARV to Ellen Browning Scripps, 22 April 1914, from EBS Archives, Scripps College Library.

45. Ibid.

46. Ibid., ARV to EBS, 9 May 1918.

47. Anna Marie Bookprinter Valentien, unpublished handwritten notes.

48. Ibid.

49. ARV to Solon, 15 April 1914.

50. *The Evening Tribune*, 25 March 1922.

51. Phyllis Van Doren, "Hidden Treasure: the Valentien Wildflower Paintings," *Environment Southwest* 494 (Summer 1981).

52. Kamerling, "Anna and Albert Valentien."

53. Apparently Valentien helped with fire damage that did occur to bird paintings by Allan Brooks stored in Scripps' La Jolla home; Scripps had commissioned Brooks to illustrate *The Birds of California* by Leon Dawson. EBS wrote to Valentien in November 1915, stating, "I return herewith Mr. Dawson's letter to you as you may want to refer to it. I shall be anxious to see your work in copying the birds." Two years later, Valentien mentions working on the Brooks bird paintings in his letter requesting payment on 4 September 1917 to EBS: "Since the matter of replacing the Bird Studies which were partially destroyed by fire, was entirely of my own suggestion and besides their not being original work by me, I feel that it would be expecting too much to ask any monetary recompense for the same." (EBS archives, Denison Library, Scripps College) In fact, there exist several paintings of birds in the collection of the SDNHM which state on the back, "by A. R. Valentien after Allan Brooks," which are explained by this letter.

54. Kamerling, "Anna and Albert Valentien."

55. *Martinez Daily Standard*, 15 November 1911.

56. Kamerling, "Anna and Albert Valentien."

57. Trapp, *The Arts and Crafts Movement in California*.

58. ARV to Solon, 12 February 1912.

59. ARV to Solon, July 1912.

60. Trapp, *The Arts and Crafts Movement in California*.
61. Kamerling, "Anna and Albert Valentien."
62. Bruce Porter to Solon, July 1913.
63. ARV to Solon, September 1913, letter owned by Pamela Bury.
64. Ibid.
65. Charles Orcutt to EBS, April 1922.
66. Anna Valentien to EBS, September 1926.
67. ARV to EBS via "Miss Loring", 19 August 1924.
68. Kamerling, "Anna and Albert Valentien."
69. J.C. Harper letter in EBS Archives, 7 April 1925.
70. Obituaries: "Death Claims Local Artist," "Albert R. Valentien, Painter, Dies Suddenly," "Noted Painter of Plant Life is Dead Here." Unidentified newspaper clippings.
71. Kamerling, "Anna and Albert Valentien."
72. ARV to EBS, September 1917.
73. San Diego Natural History Museum Research Library archives.
74. John Gonzales, Senior Librarian, California History Room, California State Library, Sacramento. E-mail to author, 22 December 1999.
75. Valentien, "Biographical notes of Albert R. Valentien."

Bibliography

Albert R. Valentien: The California Years, 1908–1925. June 2–July 3, 2000. Cincinnati, Ohio: Cincinnati Art Galleries.

Ellis, Anita. *Rookwood Pottery: The Glorious Gamble*. Cincinnati, Ohio: Cincinnati Art Museum; New York: Rizzoli, 1992.

Ertter, Barbara. "Floristic Surprises in North America North of Mexico." *Annals of the Missouri Botanical Garden* 87 (2000): 81–109.

Hardisty, Esther B. "Priceless Paintings in San Diego Museum of Natural History: The Life and Works of Albert R. Valentien." Unpublished typescript, 7 pages.

Hickman, James C., ed. *The Jepson Manual: Higher Plants of California*. Berkeley: University of California Press, 1993.

Kamerling, Bruce. "Anna and Albert Valentien: The Arts and Crafts Movement in San Diego." *Journal of San Diego History* 24:2 (Spring 1978): 343–366.

Owen, Nancy E. *Rookwood and the Industry of Art: Women, Culture and Commerce, 1880–1913*. Athens, Ohio: Ohio University Press, 2001.

Trapp, Kenneth R. *Ode to Nature: Flowers and Landscapes of the Rookwood Pottery 1880–1940*. April 15–June 30, 1980. New York: Jordan-Volpe Gallery, distributed by P. Smith, 1980.

———. *The Arts and Crafts Movement in California: Living the Good Life*. Oakland, Calif.: Oakland Museum; New York: Abbeville Press, 1993.

Valentien, Albert R. "Rookwood, or to be more concise, Rookwood Pottery." Unpublished, handwritten notes, undated, 15 pages.

———. "Biographical notes of Albert R. Valentien." Unpublished typescript from pencil notes, circa 1920, 3 pages.

Valentien, Anna Marie Bookprinter. Unpublished handwritten notes.

Van Doren, Phyllis. "Hidden Treasure: The Valentien Wildflower Paintings." *Environment Southwest* 494 (1981): 3–6.

CHILOPSIS LINEARIS
(Desert Willow, 19:37)
This shrub would be better called Desert Catalpa than Desert Willow because it belongs to the same family, as can be seen by the showy trumpet flowers of pale pink. Valentien did not paint the plant in fruit, but if he had, we would also see the bean-like pods. The common name derives from the fact that, like willows, Chilopsis linearis *is found at seeps and stream edges.*

CIRSIUM OCCIDENTALE
VAR. CALIFORNICUM
(California Thistle, 22:34)
The California Thistle is a native plant that is widely distributed in the state. It may be found in disturbed places, such as trailsides, as well as openings in woodlands and forests.

Cirsium occidentale *(22:36)*

CLEMATIS PAUCIFLORA
(Ropevine, 9:34)
Clematis pauciflora, *or Ropevine, is a woody, twining vine with creamy flowers featuring petal-like sepals and as many as 50 stamens. Fruits are characterized by long feathery styles, which give them a fuzzy appearance. Clematis vines climb by twining the central axis of their compound leaves around twigs and branches of the other shrubs nearby. A coastal sage scrub and chaparral species, Ropevine can tolerate small amounts of rainfall.*

COREOPSIS SP. *(21:41)*
This genus of showy plants in the Aster family, which usually have yellow flowers, goes by the rather unattractive common name of Tickseed.

Cornus nuttallii
*(Mountain Dogwood, 15:49)
What appear to be large petals are actually bracts—modified leaves—that serve to attract pollinators to the cluster of small flowers they encircle. Mountain Dogwood is a small tree located in forests from northern California to Canada; in southern California, it is found only at high elevations.*

CUCURBITA FOETIDISSIMA
*(Calabazilla, 14:50)
The Calabazilla or Buffalo Squash
from central and southern California
has coarse, hairy leaves that have an
unpleasant odor—hence the name*
foetidissima. *After it blooms the plant
will wither away, leaving only its ropy
dried vines trailing along the ground,
with their woody spherical gourds.
North American indigenous peoples
used the seeds for food, and all parts of
the plant are edible. The whole plant is
a source for cucurbitacins, compounds
that give the plant a bitter taste but
may be of pharmaceutical use.*

CYLINDROPUNTIA BIGELOVII
VAR. BIGELOVII
*(Teddy-Bear Cholla, 14:37)
The Teddy-Bear Cholla is cuddly only in appearance, as it is abundantly armed with spines and hairlike glochids, to the dismay of any who approach too near. Detached stem segments often litter the ground around the plant, another hazard for passersby. This is the primary method of dispersal for this species, as these loose cactus joints may root wherever they are carried.*

Cylindropuntia wolfii
(Wolf's Cholla, 14:40)
This rare cactus is characterized by extremely variable flower color, with beautiful blooms ranging from yellow to deep maroon, and all shades in between. The flowers have red filaments. Cylindropuntia wolfii *has a very limited distribution, since it only occurs in southern San Diego County and extreme northern Baja California.*

CYNOGLOSSUM GRANDE
(Hound's Tongue, 17:40)

CYPRIPEDIUM MONTANUM
*(Mountain Lady's Slipper, 7:13)
Mountain Lady's Slipper is a
threatened species of orchid found
in central and northern California
and other western states in moist
areas, dry slopes, and mixed
coniferous forests. Orchids such as
this species can sometimes take as
long as 16 years to bloom and
have very exacting requirements for
reproduction to take place. Specific
fungi are necessary for germination
to occur. These requirements,
coupled with the threats to orchid
habitat by logging and development, often result in drastically
reduced numbers of new plants.*

Darlingtonia californica
*(Calilfornia Pitcher Plant, 10:26)
The carnivorous California Pitcher Plant is endemic to the Klamath region of northwest California and southern Oregon, with a few disjunct populations. It is restricted to nutrient-poor, ultramafic soils in seeps usually called "Darlingtonia bogs." Insects enter the tubular leaves, which are nearly closed by a hood with transparent patches. Exhausted in the attempt to escape, they eventually light on the slippery wall of the leaf, where downward-pointing hairs force them into the pool of enzyme-laden water below.*

Dodecatheon clevelandii
(Shooting Star, 16:18)
Shooting Stars have basal leaves, nodding flowers with sharply reflexed purple-pink petals with a yellow ring at the base, and stamens and pistil that are clustered together in a point, which gives a beak-like appearance to the flower. For this reason they are occasionally known as Mosquito Bills. These lovely delicate spring flowers are of such a distinctive form that once seen, they are easily remembered. Shooting Stars are among the earliest of spring wildflowers to bloom in the damp, grassy meadows they inhabit.

DUDLEYA PULVERULENTA
(Chalk Dudleya, 10:28)
This chalky-leaved Dudleya is a fairly common inhabitant of rock outcrops and hard soils in the chaparral of southern California, its rosette often attaining the size of a small cabbage. The rosette of thick succulent leaves stores water, enabling this plant to continue to grow and bloom even in the dry season.

Equisetum telmateia
*(Giant Horsetail, 3:35)
Horsetails evoke artists' renditions of primordial eras—and rightfully so, as the family dates back several hundred million years. Their reproductive system is primitive, producing spores in a conelike structure at the tip of the stem. However, they more frequently multiply asexually through rhizomes.*

Eremalche rotundifolia
(Desert Five-Spot, 14:17)
This charming plant in the Mallow family has rounded leaves and flowers of pinkish-purple, with each of the five petals having a purple blotch at its base. Found in the Colorado and Mojave deserts, it extends its range into Arizona and Nevada.

Eschscholzia californica
*(California Poppy, 9:49)
Nobody viewing a rolling landscape golden with these brilliant poppies would dispute its choice as California's state flower. The California Poppy is known to occur in nearly every county in the state, as well as outside the state boundaries. A self-seeding annual, sometimes resprouting from its sturdy taproot, it readily naturalizes where garden conditions are suitable.*

FEROCACTUS CYLINDRACEUS
*(California Barrel Cactus, 14:47)
The California Barrel Cactus is
one of the most dramatic denizens
of our deserts, occasionally
reaching a height of eight or nine
feet. The pleated structure of the
ribs allows the body of the cactus
to expand or contract as the tissues
absorb or lose water. Because they
are so slow-growing, large barrel
cacti are expensive to buy legally,
resulting in a threat to wild plants
from poachers.*

Albert R. Valentien and the Southern California Art Community

Jean Stern

In the spring of 1903, Albert R. Valentien and his wife, Anna M. Valentien, went to San Diego, California for a short visit with Anna's brother Charles. They immediately fell in love with the beautiful little city and decided to stay there for the rest of the year. While in San Diego, they rediscovered wildflower painting, and Albert produced a series of 130 detailed studies of the abundant local flora. This group of paintings is now part of the collection of the Cincinnati Art Museum.

Thereafter, Albert and Anna Valentien returned to Cincinnati and continued in their longtime positions as decorators for Rookwood Pottery. In 1905, they tendered their resignations from Rookwood and Albert turned to full-time flower painting. In 1908, the couple returned to San Diego.

Soon after their arrival, Albert accepted a commission from noted philanthropist Ellen Browning Scripps to paint the entire California flora, which he estimated to be about 1,000 different plants. Scripps had a large private library in the small coastal village of La Jolla, just north of San Diego, and she wanted these paintings to be a centerpiece of the institution.

In 1911, well into the "flora" project, Albert and his wife opened the Valentien Pottery Company in San Diego. As he could only paint the flora in spring and summer, during the blooming seasons, he devoted the rest of his time to the newly formed pottery. Unlike Rookwood pottery, Valentien's San Diego pottery featured stylized sculptural designs under monochrome vellum glazes. However, for reasons not entirely clear (see article by Margaret Dykens), the pottery operated for only a brief time, and examples of their San Diego clay products are scarce.

The Scripps commission would occupy nearly 10 years of their lives, from 1908 to 1918. Anna collected and Albert painted every specimen of California plant and wildflower that could be gathered. The couple visited every part of the state, from the Sierra Nevada Mountains, to the Mojave Desert, to every valley, meadow, desert wash, and coastal plain, searching for their artistic quarry. In many cases, Albert had to look through a microscope to accurately draw the delicate parts of even the smallest plant. It was an achievement unequalled in its scope and artistic merit. Moreover, it was a scientific accomplishment that will never be duplicated, since many of these plants are now rare and in danger of extinction. In the end, the series numbered 1,094 paintings, all produced on sheets of light-green paper measuring 20 inches by 13 inches. In 1933, the Scripps estate donated the Valentien paintings of California flora to the San Diego Museum of Natural History.

When he finished the Scripps commission, Albert Valentien turned to painting landscapes, but poor health limited his sketching trips. In an interview late in his life, he stated that his only complaint was that "there are so many wonderful things waiting to be done and such little time is given to us in which to do them." He died in his home at 3905 Georgia Street in San Diego on August 5, 1925.

STUDY OF YELLOW ROSES
Private Collection

Romneya coulteri
(Matilija Poppy)
Private Collection

RANUNCULUS MURICATUS
(Buttercup, 9:29)
This buttercup was native to Europe and is now found through central and northern California. In Valentien's rendition, the faithful reproduction of a single decaying leaf only adds to the charm of the painting.

HOLCUS LANATUS
(Common Velvet Grass, 4:46)
Common Velvet Grass is widespread in the United States, although it was originally a European species. Valentien has captured perfectly the plant's soft, velvety texture.

In the early part of the 20th century, when Valentien was painting his flora of California series, southern California underwent a series of remarkable social, economic, and artistic transformations. The forces that shaped the art of southern California during this important period began a generation earlier, in Europe.

In the 1860s and 1870s, when Impressionism was flowering in France, California was yet a distant, isolated region, hazardous and time-consuming to reach. The first transcontinental railroad, the Union Pacific, was completed in 1869, with its western terminus at San Francisco. Prior to the completion of the Union Pacific, the only approaches to California were overland by horse and wagon through hostile territory, or by ship from Panama or around South America. The pre-canal Panama route necessitated docking on the Atlantic side, crossing the isthmus to the Pacific side, and boarding a ship to continue to California. A trip from the east coast to the west coast, which used to take between three and eight months, now took only seven days by train.

San Francisco, which had grown tremendously from the trade and business that had accompanied the Gold Rush, experienced a significant economic benefit from the new transcontinental railway and soon developed a sizeable resident artistic community. The direction and quality of artistic and cultural matters in a community tend to be determined by the patrons who support those activities. Patronage in mid-19th century San Francisco demanded art that mirrored European canons, especially current French modes. The dominant style in France, and indeed in upper-class America, was a derivative of the French Beaux Arts or "Salon" style. Paintings of this type were frequently large, pretentious historical and figural compositions, well suited for the grandiose homes of the San Francisco elite.

By the 1880s, another French artistic import, the Barbizon style, enhanced in America by the influence of the later Hudson River School painters, affected an entire generation of northern California landscape painters. Focusing on the landscape, the French Barbizon painters imbued their works with an active brushstroke and a dramatic

sense of light, most often energizing their compositions with vivid end-of-the-day sky effects. These artists, notably Théodore Rousseau (1812–1867), and Díaz de la Peña (1807–1876), lived and painted in the village of Barbizon, thus giving name to this style. The Barbizon style found a quick and willing group of followers in late-19th-century Europe and America.

In keeping with the French models, California Barbizon works by artists such as William Keith (1839–1911), Jules Mersfelder (1865–1937), and Julian Rix (1850–1903) were characteristically painted as dark, moody pastorals, set in forest glades, often with figures tending small flocks of cattle or sheep.

Radiating from San Francisco, the railroads steadily edged south toward the emerging cities of Santa Barbara, Los Angeles, and San Diego. In 1876, the Southern Pacific completed a railroad route between San Francisco and Los Angeles. In 1885, the Santa Fe opened a railway from Los Angeles through the Southwest to Omaha and Chicago. This route was not subject to winter closures, as was the Union Pacific Railway, which traversed the Rocky Mountains. The installation of the Santa Fe track resulted in cheap, quick availability of transportation into southern California. With a commercially viable link connecting the developing agricultural areas of southern California to markets in the east, Los Angeles experienced the first of a series of land and population booms. Within a few years, the population of Los Angeles increased from about 10,000 to more than 100,000 with the arrival of large-scale agricultural and industrial activity.

With its growth of population during the mid-1880s, Los Angeles also began to attract professional artists. By the late 1880s, several artists were counted as permanent residents. Among the most prominent were John Gutzon Borglum (1867–1941) and his wife, Elizabeth Putnam Borglum (1848–1922), Elmer Wachtel (1864–1929), and John Bond Francisco (1863–1931).

John Gutzon Borglum trained in Los Angeles and San Francisco and painted large narrative works in the Barbizon style depicting California in the accepted Western

CAREX SCOPULORUM VAR. BRACTEOSA *(Sedge, 5:18)*

From left: ERYTHRONIUM GRANDIFLORUM *(Glacier Lily)*, E. HENDERSONII *(Henderson's Fawn Lily)*, E. OREGONUM *(White Fawn Lily)*, E. CALIFORNICUM *(California Fawn Lily, 6:28)* Valentien has painted four species of Fawn Lilies on the same page, with E. grandiflorum, *or Glacier Lily, on the far left. The Glacier Lily favors sub-alpine meadows of the northern mountains of California, Canada, and Colorado. Henderson's Fawn Lily is a rare plant in California, found in the Klamath Ranges and Oregon. Several of these species intergrade with other closely related species.*

Above left: SORGHUM HALEPENSE *(Johnsongrass, 4:25) Johnsongrass is not native to California. Originating in the Mediterranean, it was widely cultivated for food and forage and has escaped cultivation, becoming a problematic agricultural weed in temperate to tropical regions throughout the world. It is common in disturbed areas and along roadsides.*

Above right: BROMUS MADRITENSIS SSP. RUBENS *(Foxtail Chess or Red Brome, 5:11) Native to Europe, the Red Brome is an aggressive, invasive grass species that has taken over large areas of habitat from British Columbia to California and Mexico. It quickly uses any available moisture and nutrients and diminishes the abundance and diversity of native annuals.*

Below left: CASTILLEJA FOLIOLOSA *(Woolly Indian Paintbrush, 19:28)*

Below right: ERYTHRONIUM REVOLUTUM *(Coastal Fawn Lily or Western Trout Lily, right) and* ANEMONE OCCIDENTALIS *(Pasque Flower, left, 2:01)*

Heuchera sanguinea
(Alum Root, 10:38)

Iris missouriensis
(Western Blue Flag, 7:09)
A native plant that is widespread throughout western North America, this iris can be a noxious pasture weed, unpalatable to livestock.

Lathyrus vestitus
(Wild Pea, 13:01)

Anyone who has grown sweet peas in their garden will recognize the Wild Pea as a familiar plant in the Legume family. In this painting, Valentien seems to delight in the beauty and intricacy of the delicate, twining tendrils, as well as the rich rosy-purple of the flowers. Lathyrus vestitus *occurs in dry, shaded places below 5,000 feet in oak woodlands and chaparral habitats of central and southwestern California.*

Lewisia cotyledon
var. howellii *(9:05)*
Named after Captain Meriwether Lewis of the Lewis and Clark Expedition, this species of Lewisia *is a fascinating plant found clinging by a very stout taproot to rocky outcrops, wedged into crevices, and in cracks on canyon walls. The flowers with their pink and white candy-striping are charming and showy against the backdrop of a basal rosette of dark green leaves. This beautiful plant is a threatened species in northern California.*

Lilium humboldtii ssp. ocellatum

(Ocellated Humboldt Lily, 6:35) Openings and meadows in pine forests and shaded stream edges are enlivened in late spring by the glowing blooms of this rare lily, arrayed on stalks that are shoulder high or higher. The name ocellatum *refers to the maroon spots on the petals, which have a dark center surrounded by a ring of lighter color.*

Lilium rubescens
(Redwood Lily, 6:41)
The Redwood Lily is a fragrant, delicate lily that favors openings in coniferous forests and dry soil of chaparral of northwestern California and the San Francisco Bay area. The flowers start out as white and then become pinkish-purple with magenta flecks. A rare species, the Redwood Lily is threatened by development, livestock grazing, and horticultural collection.

Lilium washingtonianum
(Washington Lily, 6:42)
The Washington Lily is the largest white lily native to the United States. During the heat of the summer, it blooms in the chaparral and coniferous forests of the Sierra Nevada and Cascade ranges.

LINUM LEWISII *(Flax, 13:02)*
Linum is the flax genus from which linen and flaxseed, otherwise known as linseed, oil is obtained. This species of flax features a delicate blue flower. It is widespread throughout California, found scattered among the grasses in meadows and along roadsides.

LYSICHITON AMERICANUM
*(Yellow Skunk Cabbage, 5:24)
Yellow Skunk Cabbage, despite the powerful, skunky odor that its flowers emit to attract pollinating beetles, is a lovely harbinger of spring. The strange flowers of this plant in the Arum family actually consist of a sheathing leaf-like structure called the spathe, and a dense column or spadix of minute, yellow flowers that appear just before the large leaves. Growing in areas such as swamps and stream edges, the yellow club-like flower spikes seem to float mysteriously above the water.*

Lupinus nanus *(11:41)*

Lupinus bicolor
(Miniature Lupine, 11:45)
Lupines are a confusing group, and Lupinus bicolor *is no exception since it has many named subspecies and varieties that are highly variable. Palmate leaves and an upright stalk of pea-like flowers characterize the Lupine genus.*

MALACOTHAMNUS
FASCICULATUS
*(Chaparral Mallow, 14:15)
Beginning in April, the delicate
blooms of the Chaparral Mallow
add splashes of subtle color
to the rugged green landscape of
chaparral. The name*
Malacothamnus *means
"soft-shrub"; the plant itself is
related to cotton and hibiscus.*

Mentzelia lindleyi
*(Lindley's Blazing Star, 14:31)
Lindley's Blazing Star, with its bright yellow flowers showing off an abundance of golden stamens in the center, is a stunning plant of central California found in coastal sage scrub, oak/pine woodlands and open slopes.*

Mesembryanthemum crystallinum

(Crystalline Iceplant, 8:49)
This prostrate annual, a native of South Africa, has made itself at home in California's sandy beach bluffs and coastal wetlands, in some cases crowding out native plants. What appear to be glittering dewdrops on the leaves—or ice crystals, as suggested by the plant's common name, Crystalline Iceplant—are really epidermal bladder cells that sequester excess salt, allowing the plant to tolerate saline soils.

Minuartia californica *(top)*
Saxifraga mertensiana
(bottom, 1:03)

In many cases, Valentien painted more than one species of plant on a single page. In this example, he combined a tiny plant with white flowers called Minuartia, *with a much larger species of* Saxifraga. Minuartia, *sometimes known as Sandwort, prefers sandy or gravelly slopes in central and northern California, while* Saxifraga mertensiana, *from a completely different family, occurs on mossy rocks and cliffs. In this charming painting, it appears that Valentien collected the saxifrage, mossy clump and all. This picture shows why Valentien chose an unusual colored paper for his work, since the gray-green background serves as a foil for the white flowers that would otherwise be very difficult to represent on white paper.*

NASSELLA PULCHRA
(Purple Needlegrass, 4:34)
Purple Needlegrass is a species of the chaparral, oak woodlands, and grasslands, found in most areas of California, ranging south into Mexico. It is California's best-known native bunchgrass, growing in dry clayey soils, displaying a purplish cast in spring. Extensive root systems go deep into the soil and enable the plants to weather severe droughts. Because the seeds have a long thread-like awn attached, and the seed itself has a pointed appearance, the seeds are sometimes described as "needle and thread."

A Wealth of Plants:
The Ecological and Botanical Diversity
of Southern California

Exequiel Ezcurra

I visited the Mexico-U.S. border deserts for the first time in August 1980. It was a hot, dry, unwelcoming summer when I landed, naively, in one of the most forbidding spots of the border—the Sierra del Pinacate. The midday heat was grueling. At temperatures above 50°C (122°F), life seemed almost impossible. A few weeks before, a group of 19 Salvadorans had died of dehydration and heat exhaustion while trying to cross into the United States along the burning-hot Sonoyta Valley. The visit was, for me, a confrontational encounter. I did not like the place. I found it to be dry, dusty, unfriendly, and dangerous. I went back as soon as I could to the balmy tropical highlands of southern Mexico.

On the first encounter, the border drylands overburden the heart of the newcomer with survival anxiety; deserts are hostile environments that make us feel painfully maladapted. It takes time to learn to understand this land, to appreciate its grandiose scale. The borderlands have to slowly grow on us to gain a place in our affections. They are not a place one loves at first sight. A few weeks later, however, my spirit was burning, not from the heat of the August sun but from the fire of nostalgia for the wide, open wilderness I had left behind. Like a moth subdued by the dangerous light of a glowing fire, a month later I was back in El Gran Desierto, the Great Desert. Swearing and grumbling against the heat and drought, I was unwittingly seduced by this wonderful land. A passionate fascination grew in my heart for these lands of contrasts and heterogeneity. Slowly, gradually, the dry borders won my affections. Since then, I have often returned.

The Building of Peninsular California

Geological change happens slowly, over millions of years. It is barely perceptible during the few decades of a human life span. The dynamic engines of heat and gravity are always at work, constantly reshaping the surface of our planet. Beneath the earth's thin crust, the molten magma is in slow but continuous motion. Hotter, lighter material rises to the surface, and cooler, heavier material sinks. The rising magma tends to concentrate along a worldwide system of oceanic ridges, where the crust is torn apart and lava oozes into the rift to fill the gaps. As this emerging crust gradually solidifies, it forms new ocean floor that is itself soon pulled away in opposite directions by yet more material rising to the surface from the hot mantle. This system of deep ocean rifts generates moving plates of earth crust that drift slowly apart.

But for humans, these phenomena seem almost impossible to detect. We live at a different pace. We only notice them when a volcano erupts, or when an earthquake theatrically exaggerates the slight displacement of a geologic fault, reminding us of the astonishing dynamism of the interior of our planet. Continents float on thick, burning lava like rafts of stone, but you need to be a scientist to measure this slow

MIRABILIS MULTIFLORA
VAR. PUBESCENS
(Giant Four O'Clock, 8:43)
The magenta, funnel-shaped flowers of this Four O'Clock open in the evening and close in the morning. This plant is often seen in deserts of central and southern California, Utah, and Baja California.

ERIOGONUM VIMINEUM
(Wicker Buckwheat, 8:18)
Wicker Buckwheat is common on volcanic sand and gravelly slopes from Washington to Oregon, Idaho, northern California, and northern Nevada.

progress, or a poet to imagine it. For most people, the surface of the earth is stationary for all practical purposes. It is, quite literally, firm as a rock. Most persons cannot visualize continental drift, in the same manner that a bee cannot plan on the future growth of the mesquite where it gets its nectar, or a butterfly cannot conceive of the frost of wintertime. It is simply a matter of different time scales.

Under these tremendous forces of convergence, the continents are crumpled and great mountain ranges are pushed up. The slow, almost undetectable collision of immense continental plates is ultimately responsible for almost every landform we see. While most of the continental mainland of Mexico and the United States is attached to the North American Plate, the southwestern part of California, along with all of Baja California, is a sliver of continental crust that has become affixed to the Pacific Plate and rides on it. It was slowly torn away from the Mexican mainland some 6 million years ago and is still drifting away, driven by a series of rifts that are slowly opening up the Sea of Cortez, moving the peninsula towards the northwest at a pace of about one inch per year, the rate at which our nails grow. In Southern California the drifting movement generates a long line of friction: the San Andreas Fault, where the two plates are sliding against one another.

The colossal forces in the earth's interior mantle are responsible for the incredible topographic heterogeneity of southern California and the peninsula of Baja California. Some ranges, formed by highly weathered, rounded granite boulders, remain in the region as a geologic memory of the continental split. Others were formed by volcanic material that surfaced during the separation of the landmasses. Certain other landforms developed very recently, during the Ice Ages, as alternating wet and dry periods left behind their imprint in the form of large sedimentary deposits.

It is fascinating to stand at the eastern slope of the mountains of San Diego County and look at the badlands of Anza-Borrego—with one's feet on rounded boulders of Cretacic granite, almost 100 million years old, and one's eyes looking down into

eroded mud deposits from the Pleistocene age, less than 2 million years ago. Under one's feet lies the time of the dinosaurs, and down in the valley, the alluvial badlands of the recent geologic past—the age of the great reptiles and the age of the great mammals, side by side. Here are two histories, millions of years apart, written in mud and stone.

Canyons, Dunes, and Grinding Stones

The geology of San Diego County is like an open book; the history of the region is written everywhere: in the soil, in the rocks, in the sedimentary deposits, in the landforms. The old sedimentary terraces of the coast contain a layer of alluvial deposits, rich in estuarine and wetland fossils of the Pleistocene Epoch. The rounded alluvial stones of these deposits tell us the stories of great rivers that once reached the bay, depositing rounded boulders of reddish rhyolite that came from mountains now in southern Sonora. The brightly colored stones are a memory of the region's past, more than 6 million years ago, when the peninsula was attached to what is now the Mexican mainland.

To the west, on the other side of the granite divide, the drier parts of the county show some curious rock formations that seem to have been laid carefully on the ground, side by side, by the skillful hand of an invisible artisan. Known as "pavements," these surfaces are the result of the slow wind erosion of the finer soil particles. They tell us the story of the Lower Colorado Valley desert. As the particles were blown away, the larger stones remained, arranging themselves in a single, neatly laid layer. Thousands of years of winds and drought have slowly built this strange landscape.

The rocks here seem to have been varnished by some prehistoric hand with a thick coating of lacquer. Known as "desert varnish", this dark patina forms only in extreme environments—such as very dry deserts or high mountains—in which the absence of microorganisms and water allows the accumulation of amorphous silicates and

Dendromecon rigida
(Bush Poppy, 9:47)
The Bush Poppy is a shrub with satiny yellow flowers and a height of up to three meters. It is found on dry slopes and washes of California and Baja California and is especially likely to be seen following burns.

Calyptridium umbellatum
(Pussy Paws, 8:50)
C. umbellatum, sometimes known as Pussy Paws, is an alpine perennial with spreading stems; it is found in sandy or rocky soils and coniferous forests, usually higher than 1,500 meters. It grows in Montana and Wyoming as well as California.

Quercus dumosa
(Nuttall's Scrub Oak, 7:36)

Lithocarpus densiflorus
(Tan Oak or Tanbark Oak, 7:45)
The Tanbark Oak is a denizen of the redwood forests and red fir forests of California and southern Oregon. Though Lithocarpus *is in the Oak family, the shaggy scales of its acorn cap distinguish this genus from that of the true oaks, in the genus* Quercus.

manganese oxides. Thanks to this natural sheen, we can date artifacts and rocks that were used by ancient dwellers.

Many thousand years ago, some of the first human settlers carved grinding holes into the granite. We call them *metates*, their name in the Náhuatl language. *Metates* were used to crush and grind seeds of many different plants, including mesquite, oak, and pinyon pine. These grinders are all over San Diego County, in the coast, in the chaparral, in the forest, in the desert. Based on *metates* and other artifacts, we can locate the old campfires of prehistoric inhabitants. It has always been a source of bewilderment to me to see so many sites in the hot desert, when the cool, protecting forests are so near. What rare calling led some of the first immigrants to this region to settle in these harsh drylands, where so few dare to live today? How did they survive the extreme heat and drought? Every time I visit the desert, these questions stay floating in my head, like a mirage in the hot, turbulent midday air.

Some days, the heat in the desert here is so great that the rocks fracture like brittle crystal glass. Walking in the sierras, sometimes you can hear the sounds they emit: first they make a high-pitched screech, and then, crack! they break into smaller pieces. Geologists call this phenomenon "thermoclastism"—when the rocks break as a consequence of elevated temperatures. On the rare occasions when I have heard one of those cracks on a hot summer day, I felt the earth was getting a little bit older, a little bit more experienced. A new scar had appeared on the old weather-beaten face of the desert. A new story had been recorded on the landscape, waiting for some devoted scientist to interpret it in the future.

To the east, San Diego County ends in a sea of deep sediment. Further east lies a sea of dunes; 4,000 square kilometers of sand of continental origin. Ronald Ives, an Arizona explorer who devoted his life to investigating and discovering this region, was the first to realize that these sands derived from sediments accumulated in the lower basin of the Colorado Valley, which dried up at the end of the last glaciation,

some 15,000 years ago, forming a thick deposit thousands of meters deep. From this immense sedimentary mantle, the dunes started their slow eastward march, driven by the prevailing winds. It seems almost magical to think that these gently moving dunes of soft, rounded forms are, in part, rocks of the Grand Canyon, eroded by water, transported by the river, silted, dried up, then lifted by the winds, sifted into sand, and finally deposited in the desert. A long way indeed.

WINTER RAINS AND LEATHERY LEAVES

But in San Diego County, the present is as fascinating as the past. Up in the mountains, forests whisper into the breeze the murmur of oak leaves and pine needles. Down in the valley, the plains of the Lower Colorado Valley harbor one of the driest deserts in North America, dotted in the distance by the amazingly regular pattern of creosote bushes. To the west, large expanses of chaparral roll down into the Pacific coastal lowlands. On the drier eastern slope, a succession of scrubs covers the incline with juniper, Our Lord's Candles, smoke trees, and barrel cacti. Standing on the watershed divide of these mountains, one can see ecosystems and life-forms that normally lay thousands of miles apart: tough-leaved chaparral resembling the Mediterranean maquis or the South African *fynbos*; small-leaved desert scrub, with creosote and burro bushes, similar to the South American *monte*; mountainous sky-islands, with temperate relicts of boreal pine and oak; semi-arid slopes with juniper; fog-harvesting, succulent rosette plants; and giant barrel cacti. I can imagine very few places in the world that show such an amazing heterogeneity as this region. Like a true antediluvian ark, Southern California repeats on a smaller scale many of the ecosystems of North America in an amazingly small stretch of land. Because of this heterogeneity, San Diego County is one of the most important hotspots of biological diversity in North America.

Just as the thermal energy contained in the earth's interior mantle has given shape to the regional landscapes, the energy of the sun is the driving force that moves the

PINUS ATTENUATA
(Knobcone Pine, 4:03)
The Knobcone Pine has long, oval-shaped cones that usually bend downward and encircle the stem. This pine is well adapted to fire, since cones may stay closed on the tree for as long as 30 years, until they are opened by heat generated by fire. New pine seedlings may then germinate for several years afterward. The Knobcone Pine ranges from Oregon to southern California and Baja California.

HESPEROYUCCA WHIPPLEI
(Our Lord's Candle, 6:44)
This chaparral plant blooms once and then dies. After several years of growing a rosette with sharp, rigid leaves, it sends up a stalk of up to eight feet and produces hundreds of creamy flowers. The flowers are pollinated by a moth that then lays its eggs within the ovary. The larvae grow there, eating a portion of the developing seeds.

COREOPSIS MARITIMA
(Sea Dahlia, 21:38)
Sea Dahlia is restricted to sea bluffs and scrub immediately adjacent to the coast in San Diego County and northern Baja California. Its limited distribution gives it sensitive species status.

CALOCHORTUS CONCOLOR
(Golden-Bowl Mariposa Lily, 6:06)
The bright yellow petals of C. concolor *have dark red blotches near the base, with hairs near the nectaries. A chaparral or pine forest species, it is found on dry, granitic slopes of the San Bernardino mountains and the Peninsular Ranges south into Baja California.*

atmosphere and oceanic currents. However, because of the fluid nature of water and air, as compared to the sluggish viscosity of the earth's magma, climatic and ecological change may be observed along much shorter periods of time, often from one year to the next. In southern and Baja California, the effects of the global circulation of air and sea are particularly striking.

The North Pacific Ocean has a system of currents that circulate clockwise. The equatorial current hits the Asian continent and is deflected northeast. Part of this flow is in turn circulated southward along the coast of North America, where it is known as the California current. This stream, which runs from north to south along the coast of North America, is in turn deflected westward by the rotational movement of the Earth to form the equatorial current, starting the whole cycle again. The deflected surface layers of the California current are replaced by an upwelling of deeper cool water that is transported upward from the nutrient-rich layers of the ocean floor, bringing fertility to the surface. Thus, the cold oceanic currents associated with the ocean's upwelling are the major cause of the great productivity of the regional sea.

But the cold seawaters of southern California are also the major cause of the summer drought and general aridity of the land, as the moisture-laden northwesterly winds from the cold Pacific heat up and dry as they run into the warm coastal plains. Only in winter and spring does the land cool sufficiently so as to cause atmospheric condensation and, in consequence, precipitation. Because this particular pattern of summer drought and winter rain dominates the coasts around the Mediterranean Sea in Southern Europe, the areas of the world that show this type of seasonal variation are called "mediterranean" regions. Winter rains sustain the Californian chaparral, a unique evergreen scrub adapted to summer drought. Like other mediterranean scrubs in other parts of the world, chaparral shrubs have tough, leathery, perennial leaves. For this reason, the plant is also known as a "sclerophyllous" scrub, from the Greek *scleros* (hard) and *phyllum* (leaf).

Sclerophylly, or leathery-leaf syndrome, allows perennial shrubs to use a rather narrow window of opportunity for growth. During winter, moisture accumulates in the slopes of the mountains, but the weather is too cold for plant growth. During summer, the temperature is adequate but the soil is too dry. Only during spring, when temperatures start to rise and moisture is still present in the ground, can the shrubs grow adequately. Under these conditions, retaining the leaves from the previous year gives the shrubs an early start and a competitive edge. But in order to live on until the next rainy season, these same leaves have to survive the dry California summer, when no rains occur and the soil is hard and bone dry, like an adobe brick. To avoid water loss during the hot season, the chaparral shrubs have developed leaves with a thick, leathery epidermis and few, small stomata, the pores through which leaves breathe and fix carbon dioxide.

Tough leaves, however, are not the only mechanism that helps plants efficiently survive the summer drought. The mediterranean scrubs of Southern California are also amazingly rich in short-lived spring plants, or spring ephemerals. These plants survive the unforgiving dry summer in the form of seeds, bulbs, or tubers, and quickly resprout during the narrow window of opportunity that the Pacific coastal spring provides. In stark contrast with the evergreen shrubs, their leaves are soft and tender, and their stomata are large, allowing the plants to grow very fast when conditions are adequate. Summer ephemerals are fast growers and even faster reproducers. The evolutionary fitness of ephemerals depends on seed production, which in turn depends on quick flowering and efficient pollination. Abundant and successful spring sex, in short, is the key to the success of this life-form. And, as expected, the ephemerals of San Diego County provide a veritable orgy of flowers that carpet the fields during moist springs.

It is amazing how global forces have so evidently shaped the unique life-forms here through natural selection and the slow workings of evolution. The coastal upwellings

PELLAEA ANDROMEDIFOLIA
(Coffee Fern, 3:26)
Coffee Fern gets its name from its mature, leathery leaflets, which are about the same size, shape, and color as coffee beans. It favors dry, rocky canyons from the northern coast of California south into Baja California.

ARGEMONE MUNITA
(Chicalote, 9:44)
This prickly poppy, known as Chicalote, blooms in late summer in open areas of California and Baja California.

Rumex salicifolius
var. salicifolius
(Willow Dock, 8:24)
In California, Nevada, and Baja California, this form of Dock is likely to be found in either montane or moist coastal areas.

Eriogonum thurberi
(Thurber's Buckwheat, 8:17)
The genus Eriogonum, *known as Wild Buckwheat, is a vast and confusing group; it has more species than any other genus in California. E. thurberi grows in sand or gravel of the Mojave and Sonoran Desert into Arizona, New Mexico, and Mexico.*

of the Pacific Ocean are basically the driving force behind all these wonderful adaptations. But weather here is anything but constant. During El Niño years, random variation in the Earth's flow of air weakens the trade winds, and the equatorial westward currents decrease. Instead of flowing towards Asia, warm oceanic waters accumulate in the coast of the American Continent, and the California Current loses momentum. The upwelling of nutrient-rich waters decreases, and the sea becomes warmer. Marine productivity declines, but the land is soaked by the abundant rainfall that originates from the now-warm ocean waters. During these anomalous climatic pulses, the famine of the sea is also the feast of the land, and the frenzy of spring growth reaches untold proportions.

Splendid Isolation

The term "peninsula" comes from the Latin for "almost an island." Few places on earth are so true to their etymology as Baja California and Southern California. All along the region, the driving theme is insularity: during the last 6 million years the Sea of Cortez and the lowlands of the Lower Colorado Valley have kept the long and dry peninsula separated from the mainland. The mountains of Southern California, in turn, have kept the chaparral and coastal sage scrub growing in their coastal isolation, separated from the Sonoran Desert not only by granite but also by a unique climate of winter rains. The natural history of this region is the tale of the deep causes for the diversity of life on Earth. On this territory of secluded landscapes that keep in solitude the genetic secrets of their founding life-forms, smaller patches of insularity are superimposed on even smaller scales. Marine islands, high mountains, palm oases, and coastal estuaries all represent fragmented habitats that repeat the isolation theme on smaller and smaller scales.

Rainfall in Southern California is scanty and often unpredictable. When it rains, a pulse of life makes the arid landscape truly vibrate with activity. Not only plants,

but also many other organisms are well adapted to these short-lived cycles of abundance. The annual plants survive for years as seed, but when it rains, they carpet the desert and chaparral like a garden of flowers. Other organisms, instead, store water to survive times of drought. Cacti have large succulent stems, where they store last year's rainwater like a memory. To defend their watery tissues from thirsty herbivores such as bighorn sheep, mule deer, jackrabbits, and rodents, cacti have developed formidable spines and toxic compounds. The flowers, in contrast, produce abundant nectar to bribe their pollinators into their role as sexual mediators.

Since annual plants—such as the evening primrose (*Oenothera deltoides*), the California poppy (*Eschscholzia californica*), and the sand verbena (*Abronia villosa*)—produce so much seed, and since the perennial plants—such as cacti, creosote bushes (*Larrea tridentata*), and laurel sumac (*Malosma laurina*)—are formidably defended by spines or toxic compounds, the trophic chain of the dry scrub is chiefly based on the consumption of seeds, which are non-toxic, easily stored, and by far the most abundant resource in times of drought. Granivory, and not herbivory, is at the base of the drylands' food chain. Kangaroo rats, pack rats, ants, and seed-eating birds such as quails all depend on the consumption of seeds for their survival. These granivores, in turn, serve as primary prey for the stealthy predators of the region's dry scrubs, such as coyotes, owls, kestrels, and rattlesnakes, which prey on birds and rodents, and horned lizards, which consume ants.

Other, larger herbivores, like the pronghorn antelope, the bighorn sheep, and the desert gopher tortoise, consume green foliage during wet periods but can evade the effects of prolonged drought. When the plants dry up, pronghorns migrate in search of moisture pockets, bighorns ascend to the higher slopes searching for elevations where moisture has accumulated, while the tortoises enter into a state of torpor, lowering their metabolic rates until the next pulse of rain brings another boom of growth and production to the desert.

ESCHSCHOLZIA CALIFORNICA
(*California Poppy, 9:48*)
This painting shows some of the variability in the color of California Poppies, which are typically orange, but can range from white to cream to yellow.

OPUNTIA LITTORALIS
(*Coast Prickly-Pear, 14:43*)
This sprawling prickly-pear is found in the coastal sage scrub and chaparral. Its juicy red-purple fruits are edible once the spines are removed.

Above left:
RANUNCULUS SP.
(Buttercup, 9:31)

Above right:
SCOLIOPUS BIGELOVII *(6:50)*
This very unusual-looking plant of redwood forests is called Scoliopus, or "crooked foot," because of its strangely twisted and recurved pedicels. The leaves are mottled, and the flowers are noteworthy for their unpleasant odor.

Below left: HESPEROSTIPA COMATA SSP. INTERMEDIA
(Needle and Thread, 4:33)
This grass of the High Sierras and Rocky Mountains is found in pinyon/juniper woodlands as well as coniferous woodlands.

Below right: THELYPTERIS PATENS VAR. PATENS *(3:32)*

Above left: ATRIPLEX HYMENELYTRA
(Desert Holly, 8:34)
Valentien demonstrates the silvery aspect of this plant of alkaline or saline soils, often found in deserts of the southwest United States and Mexico.

Above right: CHEILANTHES NEWBERRYI *(Cotton Fern, 3:17)*
Valentien has chosen to paint this fern of dry, granitic outcrops in situ. The leaflets have a gray-green cast, mostly from dense, minute hairs, white to tan in color, which give them a felt-like texture. This fern is found only in southwestern California and Baja California.

Below left: PLATANTHERA LEUCOSTACHYS
(White-Flowered Bog Orchid, 7:15)
White-Flowered Bog Orchids are found in wet, open areas and meadows in California as well as Alaska, Montana, and Utah.

Below right:
VIGUIERA LACINIATA
(San Diego Sunflower, 21:25)

These cycles of rainfall and drought, and the landscape mosaic of granite, lava, mudstone, and sand, are what make these landscapes one of the most rapidly changing and extraordinary places on earth. The beauty of this wilderness is rough and difficult to understand. It gets under our skin very slowly, as we unveil and understand the mysteries of these changes, the deep causes of the region's heterogeneity, the roots of its diversity.

Of Numbers, Memories, Chance, and Needs

Isolated environments are miniature universes, little self-contained cosmos. In isolated habitats, the complex pathways of natural selection operate with their own tempo, in unique modes. Isolation promotes the evolution of various life-forms, and yields with time singularly evolved descendants of the original species that colonized the area. Each fragmented environment is a unique result of chance and necessity, of random foundations and subsequent adaptation. In each isolated ecosystem, the species and their DNA carry the genetic secrets of their founding life-forms. The organisms that arrived thousands or millions of years ago have evolved separately in each isolated fragment, and have diversified to occupy all possible niches. The history of each fragment is written in the species' genes, in the natural history of its flora and fauna, in the endemisms that colonize it.

We biologists are fascinated by numbers. We love counting living things, classifying them, putting them in wooden drawers, and sometimes also in intellectual drawers, all neatly tucked up. The numeralia for Southern California yields some impressive counts: San Diego County alone harbors some 2,132 species of wild plants. The southern peninsular ranges of California (basically, San Diego County, Orange County, and the mediterranean ecosystems of northern Baja California) contain almost 60 percent of the 4,426 species that compose the total flora of the California Biotic Province. Almost 50 percent of the flora of Southern California—some 1,000 species—is

SPARTINA FOLIOSA
(*California Cord Grass, 4:49*)
California Cord Grass is found along beaches, salt marshes, and mudflats of the California and Mexican coast. Spartina *is a halophyte, or salt-tolerant plant. This species is able to survive when submerged at high tide because its stems have special cells that carry oxygen down to its roots.*

MONOPTILON BELLIOIDES
(*Desert Star*) and LANGLOISIA SETOSISSIMA SSP. SETOSISSIMA
(*Bristly Langloisia, 2:10*)
These two diminutive desert inhabitants are good examples of the kinds of plants Valentien had to examine carefully with a magnifying glass before attempting to paint them accurately. Bristly Langloisia has lavender to blue flowers and is common in desert flats, slopes, and washes east of the Sierra Nevada, and in Arizona, Nevada, and Mexico. Monoptilon bellioides *is a spreading, prostrate member of the Daisy family found in the deserts of California, Utah, Arizona, and Mexico.*

endemic to the regional ecosystems of the southern peninsular ranges and the Lower Colorado Valley. Southern California, we are all proud to announce, is a biological hotspot; it is one of the places in the United States that has the highest level of biological richness. Furthermore, faithful to its island-like origin and its incredible level of ecological fragmentation, Southern California is full of endemism, rarity, and extinction risks.

This accounting, however, is something like the financial inventory or balance sheet of nature; it tells us (more or less) exactly what is growing out there. It is a necessary exercise, but an impersonal one. The numbers of biological diversity do not reflect the dangers, the risks, and the furies that are hidden behind the slow, tortuous process of accumulation of biological wealth. These numbers say nothing about how all these species arrived in this island-region and about the animals that transported them; the cold numeralia does not speak to us about the failures, the deaths, the extinctions; it tells us nothing about the triumphs of emancipation, the random turns of sheer luck, the survival capacity of some of the extant species. Much more fascinating than the accounting of biodiversity is the history behind it, those sagas of colonization, survival, and co-evolution that we barely imagine.

Some species of tropical origin were possibly already in the peninsular island when it separated from mainland Mexico, and stayed here, alone, isolated, drifting in their stone raft, in their own ark of gray granite. Over millions of years, they evolved and became adapted to the new island conditions, until it docked against the Transversal Ranges of California and started jolting along the San Andreas Fault. A new wave of invasion must have followed then, with myriad temperate species coming in, more tolerant to freezing and more adapted to winter rains. As the mountains formed, seaside stretches became isolated again, governed by coastal fogs, winter rains, and mild maritime weather.

Then came the Ice Ages, a 2 million-year period in which the planet went through a series of long glacial events that covered most of North America under a massive ice

SIDALCEA DIPLOSCYPHA
(Fringed Checker Mallows, right)
and TRITELEIA HYACINTHINA
(White Brodiaea or White Hyacinth, left, 2:40)
Sidalcea, *or Checker Mallows, are annuals with many variable, confusing species and subspecies. Generally the flowers are shades of purple, rose, pink, or white.*
S. diploscypha *is found in grasslands, valleys, and open areas of woodlands.* Triteleia hyacinthina, *or White Brodiaea, is a member of the Lily family. Also known as White Hyacinth, it is found in the Cascade and Sierra ranges of California north to Idaho and Vancouver Island. It grows in open grasslands where the soil is temporarily wet, such as around vernal pools.*

ERIOGONUM INFLATUM
(Desert Trumpet, 8:13)
The Desert Trumpet has a strange appearance due to the inflated swellings below the nodes of its inflorescence. Research has shown that the inflation is an adaptation to accommodate a buildup of carbon dioxide concentration in stems that begin photosynthesizing when the leaves wilt or eventually dry up and drop off the plant.

CUPRESSUS MACROCARPA
(Monterey Cypress, 4:16)
The Monterey Cypress is a rare tree that is native to the Monterey Peninsula but widely cultivated and planted elsewhere. In native stands, the dramatic wind-sculpted Monterey Cypress is confined to rocky, granitic soils of California northern and central coastal headlands and bluffs exposed to onshore winds.

ABRONIA MARITIMA
(Red Sand Verbena, right) and
ABRONIA UMBELLATA
SSP. BREVIFLORA
(Pink Sand Verbena, left, 8:40)
As the name maritima *suggests, Red Sand Verbena is a plant of sand dunes, found in central and southern coastal California as well as Baja California. It is a threatened species that is considered nearly extirpated in southern California. The Pink Sand Verbena, an endangered plant in California and Oregon, is an inhabitant of coastal dunes that is threatened by vehicle and foot traffic and competition from non-native species.*

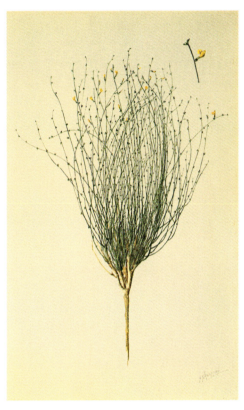

Above left:
Erodium macrophyllum (Round-Leaved Filaree, top) and Nemophila menziesii var. menziesii (Baby Blue-Eyes, bottom, 1:10)
Erodium macrophyllum, *Round-Leaved Filaree, is an endangered plant found in California, Utah, and Baja California. It is rare in southern California because it requires a crumbly clay soil in open grasslands, a habitat that is rapidly declining. On the other hand, Baby Blue-Eyes,* Nemophila menziesii, *is found in many habitats, including meadows, chaparral, desert washes, and slopes. The flowers, a favorite of many native plant lovers, can be sky blue with white centers, or blue-veined with dots.*

Above right: Lotus haydonii *(Haydon's Lotus, Pygmy Lotus, 12:22)*

Below left: Hoita strobilina *(Loma Prieta Hoita, 12:29)*

Below right: Euphorbia misera *(Cliff Spurge, 13:18)*

ERIOGONUM FASCICULATUM
(California Buckwheat, 8:08)
Widespread and very common, this semi-shrubby buckwheat is a characteristic element of many brushland and desert plant communities. Its dense flower clusters are often humming with activity, as it is a major nectar source for bees, wasps, and butterflies.

PROSOPIS PUBESCENS
(Screw Bean Mesquite or Tornillo, 11:35)

sheet for 100,000 to 200,000 years, successively followed by bouts of warm years in which the glaciers retreated north and the plains became dry and scrubby. As a result of these forces, the region is dappled by a complex series of forested mountain ranges that emerge like islands from an ocean of flat, dry sedimentary plains—known as *bajadas* in the desert or coastal terraces in the Pacific Rim—that are now covered by dry scrubs. Most of these mountains harbor remnants of the ancestral Madro-Tertiary flora, a set of temperate woodland plants that covered the region since the early Pliocene, some 25 million years ago. As the Pleistocene glaciations brought cycles of increasingly warmer and drier climates, large portions of this woodland became gradually replaced by desert communities in the east, and by evergreen mediterranean scrubs in the west. At the end of the last glaciation, some 15,000 years ago, the current scrublands took over the plains. The remnants of the ancestral woodland now survive in isolation, like antediluvian castaways, high up in the refuges of the cooler and moister mountains, known as "sky-islands."

SENSE AND SYMBIOSIS

The biology I studied in school taught me that evolution was about competition, about supremacy, about killing or being killed, about nature red in tooth and claw. But in the border drylands I developed a new view of life. Think, for example, about the mesquite, that wonderfully lush desert tree that taps water from deep aquifers. It would not survive if it did not have bacteria attached to its roots, fixing from the atmosphere all the nitrogen that the plant needs. And think about those wasps and bumblebees and beetles, which consume the mesquite's honey-like nectar and carry pollen—the sperm of plants—across miles and miles of dunes and rocks.

In the regional drylands I also learned about the barrel cacti (*Ferocactus*) and the golden-spined cacti (*Bergerocactus emoryi*), those gentle giants that establish under the fertile shade of scrub and desert legumes such as the mesquite, which protects them

from the harsh desert sun and feeds them with the nutrients derived from its root bacteria. In this region I saw for the first time the coastal agaves (*Agave shawii*), with funnel-shaped rosettes that can capture coastal fogs and thrive on atmospheric moisture without any rain. I saw the bats, which feed on the cactus and agave nectar and follow for months a botanical orgy of desert plants in flower, all the way from southern Mexico into the American Southwest.

Here I learned that in the deep caverns of the desert the bats seek refuge. They have always fascinated me. They are the cupids of the scrub: ugly, petite, unlikely gods of love that consume the sweet, sticky nectar of the agaves and carry the pollen kilometers away across the harsh desert, so that the succulent rosettes can have carnal knowledge—so to speak—of other solitary plants that are patiently waiting for these winged messengers to bring in the sperm of distant mates.

Since plants cannot walk in order to sexually encounter other plants, they have evolved some amazing adaptations to disperse their DNA. The yuccas of our region have developed a curious system in which a moth (*Tegeticula*) will travel from flower to flower laying its eggs in the flower's ovaries. In doing so, the moths pollinate the flowers, but at dear expense for the plant, as the pollination process also riddles the capsules with larvae that will eat some of the resultant embryos. Evolutionarily speaking, the yucca plants pay with some embryos for the expensive privilege of having an exclusive pollinator.

In the dry scrub I also learned that dispersal is not only about pollen (the dispersal of gametes); it is also about the scattering of seeds and propagules (the dispersal of zygotes, or whole genetic individuals). Plants will bribe their way into dispersion by offering juicy fruits, nutritious pods, or even edible grains. At first, it seems almost a mystery how grains can be scattered, as many show no clear wind-dispersal structures and are destroyed when eaten whole by their foragers. However, many plants that produce grains actually benefit from their seed consumers, which transport seeds

AGAVE DESERTI
(Desert Agave, 7:07)
Agaves bloom once and then die. However, A. deserti is a very slow-growing species and usually takes at least 20 years to flower. As the central rosette of the main plant dies, new "pups" replace it in a circle around the outer margin. The Desert Agave has been used extensively for food and beverages by desert peoples. The bright yellow, branched inflorescence makes this plant especially attractive to hummingbirds.

YUCCA BREVIFOLIA
(Joshua Tree, 6:47)
This tree gives a Dr. Seussian look to the Mojave Desert landscapes it dominates. Its bizarre form is characterized by bifurcating branching and tufts of succulent leaves. The name Joshua Tree may have been given by the Mormons who passed through the desert from San Bernardino in 1857 on their way to Utah, perhaps because the tree resembles a gesticulating desert prophet. Like other yuccas, the Joshua Tree is pollinated by a symbiotic moth.

Above left: LIMNANTHES
DOUGLASII SSP. DOUGLASII
(Douglas' Meadowfoam, left) and
CALOCHORTUS UNIFLORUS
(Large-Flowered Star Tulip, right, 1:34)

Limnanthes, *with its white-tipped yellow flowers, is most likely to be found in wet meadows or at the edges of vernal pools or streams. Since only 10–25 percent of California's original vernal pools remain, plants and animals of this specialized habitat are considered to be at risk. Like some of the other species found near vernal pools,* Limnanthes *depends on a native, solitary bee that collects pollen only from its showy flowers. These bees provide pollination services in return. The uncommon plant* Calochortus uniflorus, *known as the Large-Flowered Star Tulip, is also found in moist meadows.*

Above right: PRUNUS
ILICIFOLIA SSP. ILICIFOLIA
(Holly-Leaved Cherry, 11:24)

Below: RUBUS URSINUS
(California Blackberry, 11:08)

Above left: Prunus fremontii
*(Desert Apricot, 11:27)
Though smaller and drier than
their cultivated cousins, these
desert fruits are indeed apricots.
The spiny shrub that produces
them is found in rocky canyons
and shrublands in the deserts and
desert slopes of southern California
and Baja California.*

Above right: Fragaria vesca
(Wood Strawberry, top) and
Lotus humistratus
*(Hill Lotus, bottom, 3:08)
The Wood Strawberry is found in
partial shade in forests. Although
Valentien did not depict it in fruit,
it has recognizable red, fleshy
fruit, albeit smaller than our
cultivated varieties.* Lotus
humistratus *is abundant in many
habitats—roadsides, deserts,
grasslands, and woodlands.*

Below: Cucurbita palmata
(Coyote Melon, 14:49)

LARREA TRIDENTATA
(Creosote Bush, 13:20)
The epitome of a tough survivor, the Creosote Bush keeps its leaves through the hottest desert summers and continues to photosynthesize in the driest conditions, when many other plants would have died. Its wide-reaching, ropelike roots provide stability for sandy soils, forming shaded mounds that shelter animals like the kangaroo rat and the seedlings of other plants.

ENCELIA FARINOSA
(Brittlebush or Incienso, 21:33)
Brittlebush is one of the most reliable desert bloomers, producing a long-lasting floral display even in dry years. This plant is especially common along the edges of highways, where there is a higher level of moisture. The Spanish name, Incienso, reflects the early use of the dried resin as incense.

and store them in buried caches where the embryos that remain uneaten can safely germinate after a good rain. Grain plants do not invest in fruits because the grain itself is the evolutionary reward for the disperser. The starch- and protein-rich grains of desert ephemerals are the perfect bribe for granivores. As in the case of the yuccas and the *Tegeticula* moths, many ephemeral plants also pay with offspring for the dispersal of other offspring.

My favorite dispersal mystery, however, is that of the creosote bush, which arrived in our region from South America towards the end of the last glaciation, some 15,000 years ago. I have thought and thought and still fail to figure out how the creosote bush plant's small, wooly, non-sticky seed could have become attached to a bird and flown thousands and thousands of miles into the deserts of North America. But the simple, basic message written in the code of DNA—"replicate"—is also a very powerful one. The unspecialized dispersal syndrome of the simple seeds of the creosote bush have sufficed to expand the distribution of the species in the short evolutionary time of the current interglacial to become the ruler of the desert, *la gobernadora*—the governess— as it has been very aptly named by the Mexican ranchers of our border region.

In the regional drylands I understood the profound meaning of all those signs of nature, like the odors of the sage scrub, the brittlebush, the burro bush, the creosote bush, the desert lavender. A single rain in the scrubs is enough to unleash the volatile fractions of all kinds of aliphatic compounds, resins, steroids, pheromones, and sweet scents, small molecules that send out signals by binding to the sensory receptors of myriad animals and attracting dispersers to fruits, luring pollinators to flowers, or charming lustful males to solitary, receptive females.

In these habitats I learned to listen to sounds of all types, such as mournful songs and clicks and ultrasounds and howls and voices. These bind doves together in courtship, or keep ants on their narrow paths, or help bats navigate in the dark, or inspire coyotes to sing to the starry dome of the night, or allow us to read aloud the field notes

Above left: Asclepias eriocarpa *(Indian Milkweed or Kotolo, 16:34) Milkweeds get their name from the white latex they exude after being cut or broken. Monarch butterflies, whose larvae are immune to the toxins contained in the plant's tissues, lay their eggs exclusively on milkweeds.*

Above right: Viola ocellata *(Western Heart's Ease, right) and* Calochortus tolmiei *(Pussy Ears, left, 2:42) This charming violet,* V. ocellata, *is commonly and quaintly called Western Heart's Ease. The petals are mostly white but have yellow and purple spots on them. The top two petals are reddish-violet on the outside.* Calochortus tolmiei, *or Pussy Ears, has a bell-shaped flower that is hairy enough to suggest cat's ears. A low-growing species, it is often found in poor soil.*

Below left: Mimulus aurantiacus *(Coast Monkey Flower, 19:20) The name* Mimulus *comes from the Latin for "mimic" or "mime", due to a fancied resemblance of the open flower of some species to a comical face. The same impulse may account for this species' common name, Coast Monkey Flower.*

Below right: Mimulus guttatus *(19:23)*

PINUS TORREYANA
(Torrey Pine, 3:48)
This dramatic tree is known from only two strictly circumscribed localities: the sandstone cliffs of San Diego County and Santa Rosa Island. Due to the species' limited distribution, any threat to either population poses a serious risk to the surviving wild members. Fortunately, the Torrey Pine is in cultivation and widely planted.

PINUS TORREYANA *(Torrey Pine, 3:49)*

of Father Kino. And I learned to distinguish true colors: reds and yellows and oranges and bright blues that signal dire warnings or offer rewards and bribes to helpful animals. After a rain, the scrublands in their entirety seem to be vibrating with millions of communication signals that form a worldwide web of its own kind.

PASSION AND ALLIANCE

My work in the dry borderlands changed my stereotyped image of a competitive nature, in which killing and conquering was the rule for the survival of selfish genes. I came away with a different and somewhat opposing view: life is often driven not so much by contest, I believe now, but by symbiosis and a drive for reproduction. It is not so much about supremacy as it is about cooperation between organisms and passion of the senses.

The great wilderness of this natural region is a living showcase—a celebration, I would like to say—of two of the greatest forces that connect all life together: cooperation and passion. Their etymologies bind into one single word: compassion. By studying and protecting our natural environment we render tribute to compassion, a uniquely human attribute.

But this celebration of conservation and compassion should not be too solemn, because solemnity and pompousness are not the trademarks of true conservationists. Let me end this essay with a paragraph from Steinbeck's Log of the *Sea of Cortez*, a wonderful text from California's topmost author and Nobel laureate, written, quite fittingly, when visiting Baja California with a group of naturalists:

> We sat on a crate of oranges and thought what good men most biologists are, the tenors of the scientific world—temperamental, moody… loud-laughing, and healthy…. The true biologist deals with life, with teeming boisterous life,

and learns something from it, learns that the first rule of life is living.... He must, so knows the starfish and the student biologist who sits at the feet of living things, proliferate in all directions.... Sometimes he may proliferate a little too much in all directions, but he is as easy to kill as any other organism, and meanwhile he is very good company.

It is our responsibility to preserve these unique border environments that inspired Steinbeck to write some of his best, most brilliant, and often most humorous work, and that have inspired so many other people to write some of their best ideas.

In this wonderful border region, when resting under the immense mantle of stars, we realize that our imagination flies there like in no other place on earth. We think of the hundreds of kilometers of mountains, wilderness, and solitude that surround us, and we realize with surprise that feeling so small does not produce anguish in our hearts. On the contrary, it makes us feel valuable; it gives a meaning to our connection with this great region. The scale of our own smallness makes us feel part of a greater nature, of a greater and more compassionate society. When this apparent contradiction finds its nest in our emotions, we know the borderlands have taken hold of our hearts and our minds. The wilderness is inside us, forever. There is no way back. Whenever I travel in the scrublands of this region, I cannot help thinking about all the great naturalists who have preceded us, like Albert Valentien—the artist we celebrate in this book—and so many others, full of the excitement of discovery and the passion for observation. And I think that, decades or centuries ago, they must have felt the same exalted feelings that naturalists and conservationists feel today for the incredible wealth of life-forms and the sheer beauty of the region. Protecting this heritage is the best homage we can give them, the best way to honor their memory. ❧

CHAMAESYCE POLYCARPA
(13:16)

Above left: CASTILLEJA EXSERTA SSP. EXSERTA *(Purple Owl's Clover, left) and* TRIFOLIUM CILIOLATUM *(Tree Clover, right, 2:32)*
Purple Owl's Clover is in the genus Castilleja, *a highly variable group with lots of hybridization between species; these plants are also root parasites, extracting nutrients from other plants by means of suckers on their roots.* Trifolium, *with its three leaflets, is the clover genus, and* T. ciliolatum *is found from Baja California north to Washington state.*

Above right: NICOTIANA GLAUCA *(Tree Tobacco, 18:35)*
Tree Tobacco is a widespread non-native.

Below left: RHYNCHELYTRUM REPENS *(Natal Grass, 5:12)*
Natal Grass, as the common name would indicate, is native to Africa. Used for soil stabilization, it has become common in disturbed places, slopes, and open fields.

Below right:
BRASSICA SPP. *(Mustard, 10:12)*
The Mustard is a non-native annual that presumably arrived in California with those other European immigrants, the Spanish. It quickly became widely established in all areas except for the deserts. Its yellow flowers appear to float on slender stalks over disturbed areas and roadsides.

Opuntia basilaris
*(Beavertail Cactus, 14:42)
The flowers of the Beavertail Cactus get their vivid colors from a type of pigment known to only a few plant families. Although this cactus' lack of spines give it a benign look, the Beavertail Cactus is well armored: thousands of hairlike spines—called glochids—are borne in circular patches on the pale blue-green pads.*

PANICUM CAPILLARE
(Witchgrass, 4:27)
This native grass is found in open places, roadsides and fields throughout California north to Canada. Some species of this genus are cultivated for food or for livestock fodder. In fact, the Poaceae, or Grass family, is the most economically significant plant family of all, since it contains such food staples as corn, wheat, rice, and sugar cane.

Penstemon grinnellii var. grinnellii *(19:12)*
Notice in this painting Valentien's extremely delicate treatment of the light hitting the pale pink-to-white flowers of Penstemon grinnellii var. grinnellii, *found in the chaparral and foothills of southwestern California.*

PENSTEMON HETEROPHYLLUS
*(Foothill Penstemon, 19:11)
Penstemons, or Beardtongues, make
up a large genus of some 250
species, the largest genus of
flowering plants endemic to North
America. The genus name means
"thread-like," referring to the
thread-like appearance of the
staminode left after the petals
drop off, as seen in this painting.
A handsome plant of grasslands
and chaparral,* Penstemon
heterophyllus *with its magenta-
blue flowers has several varieties in
California.*

Phacelia grandiflora *(17:30)*
There are nearly 90 species of Phacelia *found in California and some can be difficult to identify, but this species is easy since it has the largest flowers of all (thus,* grandiflora.*) The spectacular lavender flowers have purple striping and appear in spring and early summer in oak woodlands, chaparral and sandy soils, in Baja and southern California. This plant is known as a "fire-follower," which means that it has ecological adaptations allowing it to thrive in areas that have recently been burned over. The hairs on this plant can cause a rash if they come in contact with your skin.*

PINUS PONDEROSA
(Ponderosa Pine, 3:40)
The dark green needles of the Ponderosa Pine are arranged in bundles of three. This pine is an extremely important timber tree, and is also popular as an ornamental. Ponderosa Pine lumber has a high pitch content and is very resistant to decay.
The seeds are edible as well as the inner bark, and dyes have been made from different parts of the trees by indigenous peoples. The pitch has been used for medicinal purposes, and fragrant boughs used to make bedding.

Pinus radiata *(Monterey Pine, 3:50)*

The Monterey Pine is familiar to travelers, who admire its dramatic silhouette along the windswept Pacific bluffs of central California. The species is rare in the wild, known from only three native stands in California and two on islands off Baja California. However, its numbers are great around the world, as it is a popular landscaping tree and widely planted as a timber tree in Australia, New Zealand, and other countries.

PLATANUS RACEMOSA
(Western Sycamore, 11:03)
Every aspect of this tree stands in contrast to the other elements that are typical of the regions where it thrives: from its massive twisted trunk with mottled gray and tan bark, to its large, fuzzy, deciduous leaves, to its dangling balls of fruiting heads, to the soft, dappled shade it casts. The sycamore is found in canyons, streamsides, and sandy washes of the foothills, mountain slopes, and coastal mesas of California, Arizona, and New Mexico.

POA ANNUA
*(Annual Bluegrass, 5:05)
When cultivated for lawns and pastures, the introduced Annual Bluegrass seldom manages to display the delicate array of flowering stems that it shows when it lives unmown in the wild.*

POLYPODIUM CALIFORNICUM
(California Polypody, 3:18)
The lush fern banks found on shaded canyons and streamsides seem to vanish with the arrival of dry summer days. Their leaves curl and break off at their bases as the plants await the rains of the next season. The numerous, knotty extremities of the rhizome are the "many feet" referred to by the name Polypodium.

Populus fremontii *(Alamo or Fremont Cottonwood, 7:24)*
The sight of these majestic, wide-crowned cottonwoods is always welcome in the arid west, because their presence means water is near. Ranches and homesteads were often planted with cottonwoods in order to provide much needed shade and protection from the wind.

QUERCUS CHRYSOLEPIS *(Canyon Live Oak, 7:35)*
Quercus chrysolepis, *Maul Oak or Canyon Live Oak*, *has the widest distribution of all California oaks. It is a rounded, spreading evergreen shrub or tree that grows up to 70 feet tall, with unusual specimens reported as tall as 100 feet. It is a long-lived species, with venerable individuals estimated as old as 300 years. The leaves are a glossy green above and golden yellow underneath, with leaves and branches forming a dense canopy that may almost touch the ground. The acorns are robust and feature thick, corky caps. Canyon Live Oak woodlands provide important habitat and food sources for many species of birds and mammals. Steep rocky slopes, arroyos, dry washes, chaparral and mixed-evergreen forests are preferred habitats.*

Quercus kelloggii
(California Black Oak, spring, 7:32)
The California Black Oak is a sturdy tree with dark bark and deciduous leaves that turn bright yellow in the fall. In the spring, it produces its tender young leaves along with dangling catkins of pollen-producing flowers.

Quercus kelloggii
(California Black Oak, fall, 7:33)

QUERCUS LOBATA
*(Valley Oak or Roble, 7:38)
This massive monarch of the oaks seems almost to hover, holding its broad branches barely above the grasses of the fertile cattle-grazed valleys and rolling hills of central California. Many of the state's historic trees are Valley Oaks, a fact that is explained by their long life and imposing stature.*

RHODODENDRON OCCIDENTALE
(Western Azalea, 16:05)
These beautiful azaleas, with their white flowers having one petal with a yellow blotch at the base, can be a welcome surprise when hiking along woodland streams, seeps, or moist areas of coniferous forests in California and Oregon in late spring or early summer. The same places often harbor columbines and tiger lilies, making them a delightful early summer destination.

The Importance of Global Biodiversity

Peter Raven

In the 4.5 billion-year history of our planet and the 3.5 billion-year history of life on Earth, organisms have existed on land for only 430 million years. Following the great extinction event at the close of the Cretaceous period 65 million years ago, when two-thirds of all species were eradicated, the number of species of terrestrial organisms gradually crept back upward. Our ancestors evolved into the genus *Homo* about 2 million years ago, and further evolved into *Homo sapiens* about 500,000 years ago.

So, while we are relatively new to the planet, its other complex biological communities have been developing over periods of millions of years. Humans, in turn, have only been developing agriculture for about 10,000 years. When we try to replace existing biological systems with others that give us the productivity we want, we are modifying extremely complex systems about which we know next to nothing. Our challenge is to stop destroying and using up biological communities—as if they and the planet were infinite in their capability to support us—and start living in relative stability and harmony with the Earth.

First, we must address our own lack of knowledge about biodiversity. Certain groups of organisms are fairly well known. For example, we know there are 20,000 species of butterflies in the world, including about 700 in the United States and Canada and about 6,000 in Latin America. In fact, some localities in eastern Peru have 1,500 species of butterflies—twice as many in a single square mile as in the United States or Canada.

Similarly, we know of about 420,000 kinds of flowering plants. More than 30,000 of these are orchids, which are almost entirely tropical. Fewer than 300 orchid species are native to the United States and Canada, but they, like most other flowering plants, have been named and catalogued to some degree.

Likewise, all groups of vertebrates are relatively well known, excluding the freshwater fishes of South America; at least several thousand of these species have never been catalogued. But of the estimated 45,000 types of vertebrates in the world, aside from those South American fishes, we have named and catalogued 90 percent.

Yet, there are many groups of organisms that are poorly known. Of the world's 1.7 million described species, nearly half are insects. We estimate that there are in fact several million types of insects, but only 750,000 of them have been described. In mites—a large order of arthropods related to insects—there are 35,000 described species out of an estimated million species. For nematodes, 500,000 to 750,000 species are estimated to exist, but only 13,000 of them have been named.

And finally, let us consider fungi. There are 70,000 described species of fungi out of what may be a total of 1.5 million. Those million and a half species of fungi, along with bacteria, are the primary decomposers in the biosphere. They are present on the

PYROLA PICTA *(White-Veined Wintergreen, right),* LEWISIA REDIVIVA *(Bitter Root, center),* CEPHALANTHERA AUSTINAE *(Phantom Orchid, left, 2:47)*
Pyrola picta, or White-Veined Wintergreen, is common in dry Ponderosa pine forests. L. rediviva is Bitter Root, which refers to the roots that once provided food for Native Americans. If the roots were harvested after the plant had flowered, they were bitter to the taste. The genus is named after Meriwether Lewis of the Lewis and Clark Expedition, who first discovered the plant in Montana. Cephalanthera austinae, or Phantom Orchid, is often found growing in rich soils and leaf litter of coniferous or mixed evergreen forests from California to British Columbia and Idaho.

CICHORIUM INTYBUS *(Chicory, 20:07)*
Chicory is a perennial that grows from a deep taproot; roasted roots have been used as a substitute or flavoring for coffee. A plant of roadsides and waste places, it is native to Eurasia, although it is now widespread in North America.

roots of nearly 80 percent of all flowering plants, playing a vital role in the transfer of nutrients. Fungi are also quite useful in industrial processes, as sources of antibiotics, and as primary ingredients in beer, wine, and bread. Even so, there are probably fewer than 20 people in the United States studying the systematics of fungi. Given these facts, we are unlikely to gain comprehensive knowledge of fungi anytime soon.

My best estimate is that something like 15 million species exist, other than bacteria and viruses. This is smaller than some estimates, but still suggests that we have named only one-eighth of the world's total biological diversity. This problem is even worse when one considers that nearly a million of the 1.7 million named species occur in temperate regions like the United States, Canada, Europe, Japan, and Australia, leaving only 700,000 named species in all of the tropical regions. In reality, there are probably 10 million or more species of organisms in the tropics, which means that we have named fewer than 5 percent of them.

In the summer of 1992, the Vu Quang ox—*Pseudoryx nghetinhensis*, a 200-kilogram mammal with horns about one-half meter long—was discovered in the forests of Central Vietnam. The fact that an animal this large was never seen prior to 1992 is the best proof I can offer that we know hardly anything about life on Earth, even in groups of organisms that we consider to be well known. And if we know so little about the types of organisms in the world, consider how little we know about the relationships between those organisms, especially in the tropics. Whatever we know about a community is based on our knowledge of no more than half of the organisms and only a tiny fraction of the ecological relationships. This is very little information indeed.

WHY IS BIOLOGICAL DIVERSITY DECLINING?
There are three interconnected factors driving the destruction of biodiversity throughout the world: human population, consumption rate per person, and appropriateness or choice of technology.

About 10,000 years ago, when agriculture was first developed, the total human population amounted to a few million people. By the time of Christ, there were 130 million people on the planet. We reached 1 billion people around the year 1820, 2 billion in 1930, and 2.5 billion in 1950. From 1950 to 2020—a 70-year stretch, well within the lifespan of an individual in an industrialized country—the world population will have grown from 2.5 billion to an estimated 7.5 billion.

Another profound change is the decrease in the proportion of population in industrialized countries. In 1950, there were two people in the world for every person living in an industrialized nation; now there are four. By the year 2020, there will be five. Industrialized countries have 85 percent of the world's economy and 80 percent of the world's industrial energy—oil, coal, and gas. They have 85 percent of the iron and steel and 95 percent of the aluminum. The remaining 85 percent of people in the world have only 15 percent of the money, 5 to 6 percent of the aluminum, and 15 percent of the iron and steel.

Our contribution to pollution is proportional to our control of the economy and natural resources. The United States wastes more energy per capita than the citizens of any other nation on earth. Americans use twice as much energy per capita as people in Sweden, Germany, or Switzerland do. If the United States still had the population it had in 1943—about 135 million, instead of the 280 million it has now, or the 350 million it will have by the middle of the 21st century—it could waste as much energy per capita as it does now and not have to import any oil. It would not have to burn coal or use nuclear energy. It would not have to drill around its shores. It would not have to practice energy conservation. The doubling of the country's population since 1943 is precisely what has brought about a preoccupation with foreign oil and the use of inappropriate or polluting forms of energy. Basically, Americans are living at a standard that is 30 to 40 times that of most people in the world, and they are using 30 to 40 times as much energy per capita.

CRYPTANTHA RACEMOSA
(17:46)

LAYIA PLATYGLOSSA
(Tidy Tips, 22:01)
This genus was named after George Lay, a 19th-century English plant collector. Tidy Tips, aptly named after their cheerful, yellow ray flowers with white tips, are found in many habitats from northwestern California and the Central Valley to southwestern California. Carpets of Tidy Tips blooming in April and May present an unforgettable sight.

Lomatium lucidum *(15:43)*

Castilleja subinclusa ssp. subinclusa *(19:29)*

In terms of population control, the developing countries of the world have been consistently pursuing leveling strategies since the early 1970s. Mexico's population policy, initiated in 1971, has lowered the birthrate per couple from 4.9 to 2.9. The United States, on the other hand, has no population policy. Instead, Americans have the attitude that it is bad for a particular town or state not to grow as fast as another town or state. As long as we have that growth mentality, we will continue to damage the Earth's productive capacity at an alarming rate.

The increase in population levels throughout the world is bringing about serious problems related to the use of resources. The traditional form of agriculture in tropical forests involves harvesting the trees and burning them in small areas, using the nutrients to temporarily fertilize an area of forest before moving on to another area. But as population has grown in the tropics, the opportunity to harvest trees on a cyclical basis has disappeared. Whereas the tropical moist forest worldwide once occupied as much space as the lower 48 states, it has now been reduced to about a third of its original area. Clear-cutting is taking out an area of forest the size of the state of Indiana every year; 50 years from now, no more than 5 percent of the total may remain.

The primary forces in the cutting and permanent conversion of forests are exactly the same forces that bring about the cutting and clearing of forests in the Pacific Northwest and Alaska—namely, tax advantages given to people who take the forests and convert them into something else. The people who are gaining the most from this activity are being supported by the government. There is nothing inherently moral or immoral about that: it is the tradition. So, many people working under these traditions, along with other people who simply need to use the forest resources for survival, are reducing the forests to tiny patches.

Along with losing our forests, we are losing our topsoil. Since World War II, we have lost nearly 20 percent of the world's topsoil, and it is not being renewed at anything approaching replacement rates. Each year, we are losing an amount of topsoil

equal to that of all the wheat lands in Australia. Since 1945, we have cut down about a third of the world's forests without replacing them. We have increased by about one-sixth the amount of carbon dioxide in the atmosphere, which has set us on the course of global warming. We have destroyed enough of the stratospheric ozone layer to increase the incidence of malignant skin cancer by about 20 percent in the United States.

These actions are driving an extinction event not unlike the end of the Cretaceous period, 65 million years ago, when two-thirds of all land organisms disappeared permanently and the whole character of life on Earth changed. Ours is not a world in equilibrium. As Herman Daly put it, we are treating the world as if it were a business in the course of liquidation. The real questions before us are: How can we enter into a stable relationship with the Earth? How can we overcome our tendency to use everything up?

In terms of biodiversity, as I mentioned earlier, we do not know much about many of the world's organisms, which means that rates of extinction are difficult to compute. Yet, based on the knowledge we do have, we can estimate that about 20 percent of all species in the world will become extinct within the next 25 years. This would include about 80,000 of the 420,000 kinds of plants, 1,800 of the 9,000 kinds of birds, and 900 of the 4,500 kinds of mammals. Depending on what we decide to do, we could easily lose more than two-thirds of all the world's organisms before the end of the 21st century.

As a specific example, take Madagascar, an island off the east coast of Africa that's about the size of California. About 80 percent of the organisms that live there are found nowhere else. The island is a zone of survival for species that used to occur on the continent of Africa, as well as a place where many new species have evolved. For instance, all 45 species and races of lemur occur either on Madagascar or on a few neighboring islands; this amounts to one-quarter of all non-human primates. Due to

KECKIELLA CORDIFOLIA
(Climbing Bush Penstemon, 19:09)
This plant found in chaparral and woodland habitats of southern California and Baja California features brilliant orange-red flowers. These and other red blooms are favored by hummingbirds.

SARCODES SANGUINEA
(Snow Plant, 16:03)
Snow Plant, so-called because it often appears as the last of the snow is melting in the Sierra Nevadas, is an unusual plant found in Oregon and Baja California, as well as California. It is a non-photosynthesizing, blood-red plant that is uncommon throughout its range. Because it does not photosynthesize, it depends on decaying organic material to provide all of its nutrient requirements. When the Snow Plant begins to grow, the leaf litter and soil is lifted by the rapidly growing inflorescence and one might assume initially that it was a bright red mushroom. John Muir described it poetically as a "bright glowing pillar of fire" in 1912.

RAPHANUS SATIVUS
(Wild Radish, 10:10)
The same species as cultivated radishes, this Mediterranean native is a common weed.

ALLIUM PRAECOX
(Early Onion, 5:40)
This lovely species of Wild Onion is an uncommon plant found in southwestern California and Baja California.

heavy deforestation, every single one of those species is threatened or endangered, as judged by World Conservation Union standards. Most of Madagascar, instead of being beautifully forested, is now grassland, with introduced African mainland grasses used for grazing.

Madagascar has about 10,000 species of plants—the great majority of which are found nowhere else. The rosy periwinkle, now a common backyard plant, is native only to the island. In 1971, Eli Lilly and Company began selling vinblastine and vincristine, two alkaloids derived from this plant. Vinblastine is one of the most effective drugs used to treat Hodgkin's disease; vincristine, when used in combination with other drugs, has increased the odds of surviving childhood leukemia from 1 in 20 to about 19 in 20. Species like the rosy periwinkle are vital, and yet how will they continue to survive, given the gross alterations of their ecological communities and our very limited knowledge of global biodiversity?

Western Ecuador is another area of concern. In 1950, this region was 80 percent forested; by the early 1990s, that amount was reduced to 2 percent. An orchid found there, called *Epidendrum ilense*, has been seen exactly once in nature—on a felled tree in a pasture. One individual was collected. Fortunately, it was cultivated and is now widespread in botanical gardens. This unique case illustrates the kind of aesthetic or idiosyncratic personal reasons we sometimes have for wanting to preserve biodiversity.

We also have many scientific reasons for preserving biodiversity. Cacao, for example, the major ingredient in chocolate and a product exported worldwide, originates from the tropics. And although the United States is the world's most productive nation in terms of agriculture, all but a few of its cultivated plants were first grown somewhere else. Genetic material for enriching crop plants must be found in other countries. The only plant crop species domesticated within the borders of the United States were pecans, sunflowers, cranberries, blueberries, and perhaps some squashes. Everything else that makes up the bulk of the human food supply—wheat, potatoes, soybeans,

corn, rice, beans, oats—was domesticated and has its reservoir of genetic material elsewhere.

Zea diploperennis, a wild relative of corn, was first discovered on a mountain range near Guadalajara, Mexico in 1978 by scientists from the University of Guadalajara and the University of Wisconsin. Unlike corn, *Zea diploperennis* is perennial and has a resistance to seven of the nine major viral diseases that threaten corn yields throughout the world. Economically, the plant was a very important discovery. This unique perennial corn, with all its desirable genetic attributes, could easily have gone extinct, since its entire native range is now just one rambling pasture.

Two-thirds of the people in the world depend directly on plants as their source of medicine. For the remaining third who rely on prescription drugs, the dependence on plants is no less direct. Take, for instance, tubocurarine, a modified derivative of curare, which is a muscle relaxant used by certain natives of the Amazon in their hunting. Open-heart surgery or any other surgery requiring diaphragm muscle relaxation would be impossible without it. Most of the 20 major prescription drugs in the United States are derived from a natural product, modified from one—as are cortisone, birth-control pills, and other steroids—or synthesized based on a natural product model. For example, aspirin is manufactured from non-botanical sources, but modeled on compounds originally found in willows and other plants.

Melissa officinalis *(Bee Balm, 18:19)*

Salvia mellifera *(Black Sage, 18:13)*

WHAT CAN BE DONE TO PREVENT FURTHER LOSS?
How can we preserve biological diversity before it is lost forever? Certainly, we must focus on the intertwined problems of human population, consumption, and appropriate technology. We cannot save biodiversity without addressing social justice in the world. We cannot save biodiversity without reversing the trends of global warming and deforestation.

In turn, we depend on biodiversity to help us build stability. Organisms produce

things that human society wants or needs and that can potentially be used sustainably. Therefore, we must preserve areas that still have all their organisms intact, as natural communities—whether we know about them or not—and keep them safe as long as we can.

In addition, we need to learn more about the principles of restoration ecology, such as how organisms interact within their environment, and how cutover pastures in rainy areas become forest again. However, until we reach stability in population, consumption, and technology, we will not be able to act on a wide scale.

Another complication is that very few of the world's scientists and engineers live in developing countries. Although these countries have about 78 percent of the world's population and about 80 percent of the world's biodiversity, they have only 6 percent of the scientists. Most of those scientists and engineers live in a handful of countries—China, India, Brazil, and Mexico—which means that more than a hundred countries have no scientific or engineering establishment at all.

When a country such as the Central African Republic, Ecuador, or Peru is asked to agree to an international convention, or to leave a certain species alone, or to manage its resources sustainably, there is virtually nobody there to contribute the necessary information in a way that can be trusted by the government. These countries cannot be expected to participate in international conventions of their own free will, or even to use their resources sensibly. But perhaps, institutions and universities in the developed world can train scientists from these countries and help them confront these pervasive problems.

Our treatment of the environment is a reflection of how we treat our fellow human beings. Until we can begin to understand how other people live, we are not likely to take effective action to improve their lives. This, in turn, affects our ability to deal with the environment in a responsible and caring way. If we can learn how to deal with our local problems, then we can deal with wider problems. We can eventually come to understand that the images of the world sent back to Earth from the Apollo space mission were not some kind of cartoon; they were a reflection of the fact that the world on which we live is a finite planet, a beautiful and magnificent world, the only place where we can realize our deepest hopes and expectations. Somewhere along the way, we were deluded into thinking that the world had unlimited resources, that we had a right to deal with our planetary home in a destructive way. When we finally get past this fiction, we will be able to produce a sustainable world in which there is hope of getting beyond these next few hundred years to some kind of peaceful, stable horizon beyond.

The world will not become a sustainable place because its people suddenly realized its importance and were all levitated toward some higher state of consciousness. Instead, the world will become a better place because individuals and groups of individuals chose to commit themselves to the realization of common goals. A hundred years from now, our world will be badly damaged, but there will be bright and beautiful spots, and there may even be spots that are rich in biological diversity. The number of areas that remain will be determined by the decisions that individuals are making now. We must all energize our commitment to the Earth with renewed action in our personal lives and in our collective lives.

Rhus integrifolia
(Lemonadeberry, 13:26)
Lemonadeberry is a handsome evergreen shrub that is common in the coastal chaparral of southern California. A waxy coating on its leaves helps to prevent water loss; this survival trait allows it to stay green through the summer. The thick, reddish fruits are coated with an acidic exudate; when mixed with water, the resulting flavor and scent are reminiscent of lemonade.

Romneya coulteri
*(Matilija Poppy, 9:45)
This rambling shrub in the mostly herbaceous Poppy family is popular in gardens because of its heady perfume and showy flowers. The flowers of the Matilija Poppy—up to eight inches across—are larger than those of any other plant native to California.* Romneya coulteri *is a fairly uncommon plant, restricted in the wild to four counties in coastal southern California.*

Romneya trichocalyx
*(Hairy Matilija Poppy, 9:46)
This poppy differs from its cousin
R. coulteri in that it has hairs on
its sepals and slightly smaller
flowers. It also has a somewhat
larger native range, from northern
Baja California to Ventura County.*

Rosa californica

*(California Wild Rose, 11:15)
Whether lining a shady
streambank or massed as a thicket
in a sun-drenched mountain
meadow, the cheerful blooms of the
California Wild Rose are a
welcome sight. Flowers are
produced from late spring through
summer, to be followed by red rose
hips that persist through winter.*

Rubus parviflorus
*(Thimbleberry, 11:09)
Thimbleberry is immediately recognizable as akin to raspberries and blackberries, and is found throughout California as well as New Mexico, Alaska and Canada. Unlike many others of these berries, however, Thimbleberry has no prickles. Although the plant has few flowers, they are relatively large compared to others typical of this group.*

SAMBUCUS MEXICANA
(Blue Elderberry, 19:44)
There is some disagreement about the edibility of the Blue Elderberry fruits. Although they are considered a food plant by Native Americans and can be cooked for pies or jelly, there are also reports of gastric upset when ingesting large quantities. This small tree or shrub in the Honeysuckle family is found along streamsides and open spots in forests throughout California and other parts of the West. It flowers in the early summer and produces fruits that are almost black but have a waxy, glaucous covering that makes them appear blue.

Sedum spathulifolium *(10:27)*
This succulent plant with bright yellow flowers and spatula-shaped leaves grows on rocky outcrops, often in shaded areas. A member of the Crassulaceae, or Stonecrop family, this species has produced many cultivars for use in ornamental rock gardens.

SEQUOIA SEMPERVIRENS
(Coast Redwood, 4:11)
Coast Redwoods reach great age and height, but their distribution is restricted to the coastal fog belt of northern California and southern Oregon. The drip of moisture combed from the fog that passes through the forest ensures that the summers will be as moist as the rainy winters, allowing the magnificent trees to grow throughout the year.

XEROPHYLLUM TENAX
(Beargrass, 5:27)
This member of the Lily family persists for several years without flowering, then suddenly gives rise to a showy flowering stalk that dies back after setting fruit. The leaves of Beargrass were used by indigenous peoples to make watertight baskets.

XYLOCOCCUS BICOLOR
*(Coast Manzanita, or
Mission Manzanita, 16:16)
One of the dominant shrubs of
coastal California, Mission
Manzanita has leaves of dark
green on the top, but densely hairy
on the bottom, so that they have a
white or gray appearance
underneath. Its smooth pinkish
bark and flowers show its
relationship to the manzanitas of
the inland chaparral communities,
but the rolled-under margins of the
leaves help to distinguish it.*

ZIGADENUS SP.
(Death Camas, 5:30)
These perennial lilies are beautiful to look at, but they contain toxic alkaloids, particularly concentrated in the bulbs. They were responsible for serious illness among members of the Lewis and Clark Expedition who tried to ingest them.

Above left:
CYPERUS VIRENS *(5:23)*

Above right:
TRITELEIA PEDUNCULARIS
(Long-rayed Triteleia, 5:44)

Below:
PINUS MONTICOLA
(Western White Pine, 4:04)
The Western White Pine has cones that are almost cylindrical in shape. Needles come in bundles of five, and mature trees have bark in rectangular plates. A species of the Pacific Northwest, the Western White Pine may live up to 400 years.

Above left:
Triteleia hendersonii var. hendersonii *(Henderson's Triteleia, left),* Triteleia ixioides ssp. splendens *(Splendid Triteleia, right, 5:43)*

Above right: Calochortus venustus *(6:10)*

Below: Sesuvium verrucosum *(Western Sea Purslane, 8:45) Western Sea Purslane is an uncommon plant that forms mats on wet or seasonally dry flats, margins of salt marshes, and in deserts. This species is found from central and southern California into Oregon and Kansas.*

Above left: CELTIS RETICULATA (*Net-Leaf Hackberry, 7:49*)
The Net-Leaf Hackberry has nubby, gray-brown bark with irregular corky ridges. The leathery leaves are dark green and display conspicuous raised net-like veins on their lower surfaces. The form of the tree is often sprawling and twisted, as shown in this image. Fruits of the Hackberry are much loved by birds.

Above right: ISOMERIS ARBOREA (*Bladderpod, 9:50*)
*Isomeris arborea, or Bladderpod, is a small- to medium-sized thickly branched shrub with inflated fruits and compound leaves with 3–15 leaflets. It occurs in semi-arid and arid conditions, such as on coastal bluffs and hills and in desert washes. This plant is in the same family as the plant that produces edible capers (*Capparaceae*), but the leaves of* Isomeris *have a strong, unpleasant odor, which accounts for another common name, Stinkweed.*

Below left: DICENTRA FORMOSA (*Oregon Bleeding Heart, 10:02*)

Below right:
BRASSICA SP. (*Mustard, 10:11*)

Above left: Dithyrea californica *(10:22)*

Above right: Lepidium fremontii var. fremontii *(10:23)*

Below left: Thysanocarpus curvipes *and* Thysanocarpus radians *(10:25)*

Below right: Dudleya cymosa ssp. cymosa *(10:31)*

Above left: Heuchera micrantha *(10:39)*

Above right: Ribes speciosum *(Fuchsia-Flowered Gooseberry, 10:50)*

Below left: Ribes victoris *(Victor's Gooseberry, 11:01)*

Below right: Chamaebatia australis *(Southern Mountain Misery, 11:07)*

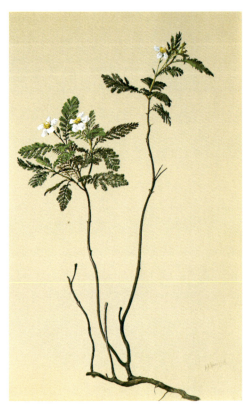

Above left: Potentilla glandulosa ssp. nevadensis (11:11)

Above right: Amelanchier utahensis (*Utah Service Berry, 11:18*)

Below left: Prunus virginiana var. demissa (*Western Choke-Cherry, 11:25*)

Below right: Cercidium floridum ssp. floridum (*Blue Palo Verde, 11:32*)

Above left:
Parkinsonia aculeata
(Mexican Palo Verde, 11:33)

Above right: Lupinus
albicaulis *(11:43)*

Below: Lupinus concinnus
(Bajada Lupine, 11:47)

Above left: Acacia greggii
(*Catclaw, 11:36*)

Above right:
Lupinus truncatus (*12:02*)

Below: Trifolium fucatum
(*12:13*)

PSOROTHAMNUS SCHOTTII
(Indigo Bush, 12:33)

Appendix

Annette L. Winner

This Appendix was taken from the database compiled for the San Diego Natural History Museum collection of 1,094 Valentien paintings. Many of the original plant identifications required updating to conform to current taxonomic nomenclature. Some of the paintings did not have plant names and lacked finite, anatomical plant detail to determine species, subspecies, or variety.

Specifics on conservation status can be found in the California Native Plant Society (CNPS) 2001 Inventory and on the California Fish and Game website (CA = all State designations, FE = all Federal designations).

The following references were utilized in determining much of the information required for the Valentien database.

Anderson, Edward F. 2001. *The Cactus Family*. Timber Press, Portland, OR

Bailey, L. H. 1949. *Manual of Cultivated Plants*. Macmillan Company, New York, NY

Britton, N. L. and J. N. Rose. 1963. *The Cactaceae: Descriptions and Illustrations of Plants of the Cactus Family*. Vols. I and II. Dover Publications, Inc., New York, NY

CNPS. 2001. *Inventory of Rare and Endangered Plants of California*. Sixth Edition. Rare Plant Scientific Advisory Committee, David P. Tibor, Convening Editor. California Native Plant Society. Sacramento, CA

Hickman, James C., Editor. 1993. *The Jepson Manual: Higher Plants of California*. University of California Press, Berkeley, CA

Jepson, Willis Linn. 1925. *A Manual of the Flowering Plants of California*. Sather Gate Bookshop, Berkeley, CA

Munz, Philip A. and David D. Keck. 1975. *A California Flora*. University of California Press, Berkeley, CA

Munz, Philip A. 1974. *A Flora of Southern California*. University of California Press, Berkeley, CA

Kartesz, John T. 1994. *A Synonymized Checklist of the Vascular Flora of the United States, Canada, and Greenland*. Vols. I and II. Timber Press, Portland, OR

Simpson, Michael G. and Jon P. Rebman. 2001. *Checklist of the Vascular Plants of San Diego County*. Third Edition. San Diego State University Herbarium Press, San Diego, CA

State of California, Department of Fish and Game, Wildlife & Habitat Data Analysis Branch, California Natural Diversity Database. http://www.dfg.ca.gov/whdab/pdfs/TEPlants.pdf. State and Federally Listed Endangered, Threatened, and Rare Plants of California. July 2003. Sacramento, CA

Wiggins, Ira L. 1980. *Flora of Baja California*. Stanford University Press, Stanford, CA

Many people have worked on this portion of the Valentien Project. I am especially grateful to Marty Blake-Jacobson, Judy Gibson, Bob Lauri, Jon Rebman, and Karen Rich for assistance with plant identification and database design.

Annette L. Winner
Botany Department Volunteer, San Diego Natural History Museum

	Scientific Name	Common Name	Origin	Status	Distribution
1:3	*Minuartia californica* (A. Gray) Mattf. (Caryophyllaceae)	California Sandwort	Native		c&nCA
1:3	*Saxifraga mertensiana* (Saxifragaceae)	Saxifrage	Native		c&nCA
1:4	*Calypso bulbosa* (L.) Oakes (Orchidaceae)	Fairy Slipper	Native		c&nCA
1:4	*Synthyris reniformis* (Douglas) Benth (Scrophulariaceae)	Snow Queen	Native		c&nCA
1:10	*Erodium macrophyllum* Hook. & Arn. (Geraniaceae)	Round-Leaved Filaree	Native	CNPS Listed	CA,BajaCA
1:10	*Nemophila menziesii* Hook. & Arn. var. *menziesii* (Hydrophyllaceae)	Baby Blue-Eyes	Native		CA,BajaCA
1:24	*Fritillaria pluriflora* Benth. (Liliaceae)	Adobe Lily	Native	CNPS Listed	c&nCA
1:24	*Dodecatheon hendersonii* A. Gray (Primulaceae)	Mosquito Bills, Sailor Caps	Native		c&nCA
1:34	*Calochortus uniflorus* Hook. & Arn. (Liliaceae)	Large-Flowered Star-Tulip	Native		c&nCA
1:34	*Limnanthes douglasii* R. Br. ssp. *douglasii* (Limnanthaceae)	Douglas' Meadowfoam	Native		c&nCA
1:36	*Nemophila maculata* Lindley (Hydrophyllaceae)	Fivespot	Native		c&nCA
1:36	*Mimulus douglasii* (Benth.) A. Gray (Scrophulariaceae)	Douglas' Monkey Flower	Native		c&nCA
1:36	*Triphysaria eriantha* (Benth.) Chuang & Heckard ssp. *rosea* (A. Gray) Chuang & Heckard (Scrophulariaceae)	Butter-and-Eggs, Johnny Tuck	Native		CA
2:1	*Erythronium revolutum* Smith (Liliaceae)	Coast Fawn Lily	Native	CNPS Listed	nCA
2:1	*Anemone occidentalis* S. Watson (Ranunculaceae)		Native		c&nCA
2:8	*Eriophyllum pringlei* A. Gray (Asteraceae)	Pringle's Woolly Daisy	Native		c&sCA,AZ,BajaCA
2:8	*Eriophyllum wallacei* (A. Gray) A. Gray (Asteraceae)	Wallace's Woolly Daisy	Native		c&sCA,AZ,BajaCA
2:8	*Glyptopleura marginata* D. Eaton (Asteraceae)		Native		c&sCA,AZ
2:8	*Syntrichopappus fremontii* A. Gray (Asteraceae)	Fremont's Syntrichopappus	Native		c&sCA,AZ
2:10	*Monoptilon bellioides* (A. Gray) H.M. Hall (Asteraceae)	Desert Star	Native		sCA,AZ,BajaCA
2:10	*Langloisia setosissima* (Torrey & A. Gray) E. Greene ssp. *setosissima* (Polemoniaceae)	Bristly Langloisia	Native		c&sCA,AZ,BajaCA
2:19	*Oenothera californica* (S. Watson) S. Watson ssp. *californica* (Onagraceae)	California Evening Primrose	Native		c&sCA,AZ,BajaCA
2:19	*Mohavea confertiflora* (Benth.) A.A. Heller (Scrophulariaceae)	Ghost Flower	Native		c&sCA,AZ,BajaCA
2:21	*Lessingia glandulifera* A. Gray var. *glandulifera* (Asteraceae)	Valley Lessingia	Native		c&sCA,BajaCA
2:21	*Lepidium flavum* Torrey var. *flavum* (Brassicaceae)	Peppergrass, Pepperwort	Native		c&sCA,BajaCA
2:32	*Trifolium ciliolatum* Benth. (Fabaceae)	Tree Clover	Native		CA,BajaCA
2:32	*Castilleja exserta* (A.A. Heller) Chuang & Heckard ssp. *exserta* (Scrophulariaceae)	Purple Owl's Clover	Native		CA,AZ,BajaCA
2:40	*Triteleia hyacinthina* (Lindley) E. Greene (Liliaceae)	White Brodiaea	Native		c&nCA
2:40	*Sidalcea diploscypha* (Torrey & A. Gray) Benth. (Malvaceae)	Checker Mallow, Checkerbloom	Native		c&nCA
2:42	*Calochortus tolmiei* Hook. & Arn. (Liliaceae)	Pussy Ears	Native		c&nCA
2:42	*Viola ocellata* Torrey & A. Gray (Violaceae)	Western Heart's Ease	Native		c&nCA
2:47	*Pyrola picta* Smith (Ericaceae)	White-Veined Wintergreen	Native		CA,BajaCA
2:47	*Cephalanthera austinae* (A. Gray) A.A. Heller (Orchidaceae)	Phantom Orchid	Native		CA
2:47	*Lewisia rediviva* Pursh (Portulacaceae)	Bitter Root	Native		sCA
2:48	*Linanthus dichotomus* Benth. ssp. *dichotomus* (Polemoniaceae)	Evening Snow	Native		CA,AZ
2:48	*Delphinium depauperatum* Torrey & A. Gray (Ranunculaceae)	Larkspur	Native		c&nCA
3:8	*Lotus humistratus* E. Greene (Fabaceae)	Hill Lotus	Native		CA,BajaCA
3:8	*Fragaria vesca* L. (Rosaceae)	Wood Strawberry	Native		CA,BajaCA
3:16	*Pentagramma triangularis* (Kaulf.) G. Yatskievych, M.D. Windham, & E. Wollenweber ssp. *triangularis* (Pteridaceae)	California Goldenback Fern	Native		CA,BajaCA
3:17	*Cheilanthes newberryi* (D. Eaton) Domin (Pteridaceae)	California Cotton Fern	Native		c&sCA,BajaCA
3:18	*Polypodium californicum* Kaulf. (Polypodiaceae)	California Polypody	Native		CA,BajaCA
3:20	*Adiantum aleuticum* (Ruupr.) C.A. Paris (Pteridaceae)	Five-Finger Fern	Native		c&nCA
3:26	*Pellaea andromedifolia* (Kaulf.) Fee (Pteridaceae)	Coffee Fern	Native		sCA,BajaCA
3:29	*Woodwardia fimbriata* Sm. (Blenchnaceae)	Giant Chain Fern	Native		CA,AZ,BajaCA
3:30	*Polystichum munitum* (Kaulf.) K. Presl. (Dryopteridaceae)	Western Sword Fern	Native		CA,BajaCA
3:32	*Thelypteris patens* (Sw.) Small var. *patens* (Thelypteridaceae)	Wood Fern	Introduced		cCA
3:33	*Dryopteris arguta* (Kaulf.) Maxon (Dryopteridaceae)	Wood Fern	Native		CA,AZ,BajaCA
3:35	*Equisetum telmateia* Ehrh. ssp. *braunii* (Milde) R.L. Hauke (Equisetaceae)	Giant Horsetail	Native		CA
3:40	*Pinus ponderosa* Laws. (Pinaceae)	Pacific Ponderosa Pine	Native		CA,BajaCA

Above left:
ASTRAGALUS LENTIGINOSUS
VAR. BORREGANUS
(Borrego Milkvetch, 12:38)

Above right: VICIA AMERICANA
VAR. AMERICANA
(American Vetch, 12:45)

Below left:
LATHYRUS SULPHUREUS
(Wild Pea, 12:48)

Below right:
LATHYRUS VESTITUS *(12:50)*

Above left: OXALIS OREGANA
(Redwood Sorrel, 13:03)

Above right: SIDALCEA
MALVAEFLORA SSP. SPARSIFOLIA
(Checker Mallow, 14:11)

Below: ERODIUM MOSCHATUM
(Filaree, 13:09)

3:48	*Pinus torreyana* Carrière (Pinaceae)	Torrey Pine	Native	CNPS Listed	sCA
3:49	*Pinus torreyana* Carrière (Pinaceae)	Torrey Pine	Native	CNPS Listed	sCA
3:50	*Pinus radiata* D. Don (Pinaceae)	Monterey Pine	Native	CNPS Listed	cCA,BajaCA
4:3	*Pinus attenuata* Lemmon (Pinaceae)	Knobcone Pine	Native		CA,BajaCA
4:4	*Pinus monticola* Douglas (Pinaceae)	Western White Pine	Native		c&nCA
4:11	*Sequoia sempervirens* (D.Don) Endl. (Taxodiaceae)	Redwood	Native		CA
4:16	*Cupressus macrocarpa* Gordon (Cupressaceae)	Monterey Cypress	Native	CNPS Listed	CA,BajaCA
4:25	*Sorghum halepense* (L.) Pers. (Poaceae)	Johnsongrass	Introduced		CA,BajaCA
4:27	*Panicum capillare* L. (Poaceae)	Witchgrass	Native		CA,BajaCA
4:33	*Hesperostipa comata* (Trin. & Rupr.) Barkworth ssp. *intermedia* (Scribner & Tweedy) Barkworth (Poaceae)	Needle and Thread	Native		c&nCA
4:34	*Nassella pulchra* (A.Hitchc.) Barkworth (Poaceae)	Purple Needlegrass	Native		CA,BajaCA
4:46	*Holcus lanatus* L. (Poaceae)	Common Velvet Grass	Introduced		CA,BajaCA
4:49	*Spartina foliosa* Trin. (Poaceae)	California Cord Grass	Native		CA,BajaCA
5:1	*Distichlis spicata* (L.) E. Greene (Poaceae)	Saltgrass	Native		CA,BajaCA
5:3	*Lamarckia aurea* (L.) Moench (Poaceae)	Goldentop	Introduced		CA,AZ,BajaCA
5:5	*Poa annua* L. (Poaceae)	Annual Bluegrass	Introduced		CA,BajaCA
5:6	*Poa fendleriana* (Steudel) Vasey ssp. *longiligula* (Scribner & Williams) R. Soreng (Poaceae)	Longtongue Mutton Grass	Native		c&sCA,BajaCA
5:11	*Bromus madritensis* L. ssp. *rubens* (L.) Husnot (Poaceae)	Foxtail Chess, Red Brome	Introduced		CA,BajaCA
5:12	*Rhynchelytrum repens* (Willd.) C. E. Hubb (Poaceae)	Natal Grass	Introduced		CA,BajaCA
5:13	*Melica imperfecta* Trin. (Poaceae)	Coast Range Melic	Native		c&sCA,BajaCA
5:18	*Carex scopulorum* Holm. var. *bracteosa* (L.Bailey) F. Herm. (Cyperaceae)	Sedge	Native		c&nCA
5:23	*Cyperus virens* Michx. (Cyperaceae)	Nutsedge, Galingale	Introduced		CA
5:24	*Lysichiton americanum* Hultén & St. John (Araceae)	Yellow Skunk Cabbage	Native		c&nCA
5:27	*Xerophyllum tenax* (Pursh) Nutt. (Liliaceae)	Beargrass, Basket Grass	Native		c&nCA
5:30	*Zigadenus* sp. (Liliaceae)	Death Camas			
5:32	*Hesperocallis undulata* A. Gray (Liliaceae)	Desert Lily	Native		c&sCA,AZ,BajaCA
5:40	*Allium praecox* Brandegee (Liliaceae)	Early Onion	Native		sCA,BajaCA
5:41	*Allium peninsulare* Lemmon var. *peninsulare* (Liliaceae)	Red-Flowered Onion	Native		CA,BajaCA
5:41	*Brodiaea minor* (Benth.) S. Watson (Liliaceae)	Dwarf Brodiaea	Native		c&nCA
5:42	*Brodiaea purdyi* Eastw. (Liliaceae)	Purdy's Brodiaea	Native		c&nCA
5:43	*Triteleia hendersonii* Greene var. *hendersonii* (Liliaceae)	Henderson's Triteleia	Native	CNPS Listed	nCA
5:43	*Triteleia ixioides* (S. Watson) E. Greene ssp. *splendens* Hort. (Liliaceae)	Splendid Triteleia	Introduced		CA
5:44	*Triteleia peduncularis* Lindley (Liliaceae)	Long-Rayed Brodiaea	Native		c&nCA
5:47	*Dichelostemma capitatum* Alph. Wood ssp. *capitatum* (Liliaceae)	Blue Dicks	Native		CA,BajaCA
6:4	*Calochortus amabilis* Purdy (Liliaceae)	Diogenes' Lantern	Native		sCA
6:6	*Calochortus concolor* (Baker) Purdy (Liliaceae)	Mariposa Lily	Native		sCA,BajaCA
6:7	*Calochortus splendens* Benth. (Liliaceae)	Splendid Mariposa Lily	Native		CA,BajaCA
6:8	*Calochortus splendens* Benth. (Liliaceae)	Splendid Mariposa Lily	Native		CA,BajaCA
6:10	*Calochortus vestae* Purdy (Liliaceae)	Mariposa Lily	Native		nCA
6:11	*Calochortus vestae* Purdy (Liliaceae)	Mariposa Lily	Native		nCA
6:13	*Calochortus macrocarpus* Douglas (Liliaceae)	Mariposa Lily	Native		c&nCA
6:17	*Calochortus venustus* Benth. (Liliaceae)	Mariposa Lily	Native		c&sCA
6:21	*Calochortus venustus* Benth. (Liliaceae)	Mariposa Lily	Native		c&sCA
6:22	*Calochortus venustus* Benth. (Liliaceae)	Mariposa Lily	Native		c&sCA
6:23	*Calochortus venustus* Benth. (Liliaceae)	Mariposa Lily	Native		c&sCA
6:24	*Calochortus venustus* Benth. (Liliaceae)	Mariposa Lily	Native		c&sCA
6:25	*Calochortus venustus* Benth. (Liliaceae)	Mariposa Lily	Native		c&sCA
6:26	*Calochortus venustus* Benth. (Liliaceae)	Mariposa Lily	Native		c&sCA
6:27	*Calochortus pulchellus* Benth. (Liliaceae)	Mount Diablo Fairy Lantern	Native	CNPS Listed	c&nCA
6:27	*Erythronium grandiflorum* Pursh. (Liliaceae)	Glacier Lily	Native		nCA
6:28	*Erythronium californicum* Purdy (Liliaceae)	California Fawn Lily	Native		nCA
6:28	*Erythronium citrinum* S. Watson (Liliaceae)	Lemon-Colored Fawn Lily	Native		nCA
6:28	*Erythronium grandiflorum* Pursh. (Liliaceae)	Glacier Lily	Native		nCA

Above left:
Ceanothus integerrimus
(Deer Brush, 13:45)

Above right:
Ceanothus pinetorum
(Kern Ceanothus, 13:48)

Below left: Ceanothus
cuneatus var. rigidus
(Monterey Ceanothus, 14:02)

Below right: Ceanothus
tomentosus *(14:03)*

6:28	*Erythronium hendersonii* S. Watson (Liliaceae)	Henderson's Fawn Lily	Native	CNPS Listed	nCA
6:28	*Erythronium oregonum* Appleg. (Liliaceae)	Oregon Fawn Lily	Native		nCA
6:33	*Fritillaria biflora* Lindley var. *biflora* (Liliaceae)	Chocolate Lily, Mission Bells	Native		CA,BajaCA
6:35	*Lilium humboldtii* Roezl & Leichtlin ssp. *ocellatum* (Kellogg) Thorne (Liliaceae)	Ocellated Humboldt Lily	Native	CNPS Listed	c&sCA,BajaCA
6:40	*Lilium parryi* S. Watson (Liliaceae)	Lemon Lily	Native	CNPS Listed	sCA,AZ,BajaCA
6:41	*Lilium rubescens* S. Watson (Liliaceae)	Redwood Lily	Native	CNPS Listed	c&nCA
6:42	*Lilium washingtonianum* Kellogg (Liliaceae)	Washington Lily	Native		c&nCA
6:44	*Hesperoyucca whipplei* (Torrey) Trelease ssp. *whipplei* K.H. Clary (Liliaceae)	Our Lord's Candle	Native		sCA,BajaCA
6:47	*Yucca brevifolia* Engelm. (Liliaceae)	Joshua Tree	Native		c&sCA,AZ,BajaCA
6:50	*Scoliopus bigelovii* Torrey (Liliaceae)		Native		c&nCA
7:7	*Agave deserti* (Engelm.) Gentry (Liliaceae)	Desert Agave	Native		c&sCA,AZ,BajaCA
7:9	*Iris missouriensis* Nutt. (Iridaceae)	Western Blue Flag	Native		CA,nMex
7:11	*Iris macrosiphon* Torrey (Iridaceae)	Iris	Native		c&nCA
7:13	*Cypripedium montanum* Lindley (Orchidaceae)	Mountain Lady's Slipper	Native	CNPS Listed	c&nCA
7:14	*Cypripedium californicum* A. Gray (Orchidaceae)	California Lady's Slipper	Native	CNPS Listed	c&nCA
7:15	*Platanthera leucostachys* Lindley (Orchidaceae)	White-Flowered Bog-Orchid	Native		sCA,BajaCA
7:21	*Salix lasiolepis* Benth. (Salicaceae)	Arroyo Willow	Native		CA,BajaCA
7:24	*Populus fremontii* S. Watson ssp. *fremontii* (Salicaceae)	Alamo, Fremont Cottonwood	Native		CA,BajaCA
7:32	*Quercus kelloggii* Newb. (Fagaceae)	California Black Oak	Native		CA,BajaCA
7:33	*Quercus kelloggii* Newb. (Fagaceae)	California Black Oak	Native		CA,BajaCA
7:35	*Quercus chrysolepis* Liebm. (Fagaceae)	Maul Oak, Canyon Live Oak	Native		CA,AZ,BajaCA
7:36	*Quercus dumosa* Nutt. (Fagaceae)	Nuttall's Scrub Oak	Native	CNPS Listed	sCA,BajaCA
7:38	*Quercus lobata* Nee (Fagaceae)	Valley Oak, Roble	Native		CA
7:45	*Lithocarpus densiflorus* (Hook & Arn.) Rehder var. *densiflorus* (Fagaceae)	Tan Oak, Tanbark Oak	Native		CA
7:49	*Celtis reticulata* Torrey (Ulmaceae)	Net-Leaf Hackberry	Native		c&sCA,BajaCA
7:50	*Asarum caudatum* Lindley (Aristolochiaceae)	Wild Ginger	Native		c&nCA
8:5	*Anemopsis californica* (Nutt.) Hook & Arn. (Saururaceae)	Yerba Mansa	Native		c&sCA,BajaCA
8:8	*Eriogonum fasciculatum* Benth. var. *foliolosum* (Nutt.) Abrams (Polygonaceae)	California Buckwheat	Native		c&sCA,BajaCA
8:13	*Eriogonum inflatum* Torrey & Frémont (Polygonaceae)	Desert Trumpet	Native		c&sCA,AZ,BajaCA
8:17	*Eriogonum thurberi* Torrey (Polygonaceae)	Thurber's Buckwheat	Native		c&sCA,AZ,BajaCA
8:18	*Eriogonum vimineum* Benth. (Polygonaceae)	Wicker Buckwheat	Native		nCA
8:24	*Rumex salicifolius* J.A. Weinm. var. *salicifolius* (Polygonaceae)	Willow Dock	Native		CA,BajaCA
8:34	*Atriplex hymenelytra* (Torrey) S. Watson (Chenopodiaceae)	Desert Holly	Native		c&sCA,AZ,BajaCA
8:40	*Abronia maritima* S. Watson (Nyctaginaceae)	Red Sand Verbena	Native	CNPS Listed	c&sCA,BajaCA
8:40	*Abronia umbellata* Lam. ssp. *breviflora* (Standley) Munz (Nyctaginaceae)	Pink Sand Verbena	Native	CNPS Listed	c&nCA
8:43	*Mirabilis multiflora* (Torrey) A. Gray var. *pubescens* S. Watson (Nyctaginaceae)	Froebell's Four O'Clock	Native		c&sCA,AZ,BajaCA
8:45	*Sesuvium verrucosum* Raf. (Aizoaceae)	Western Sea Purslane	Native		CA,BajaCA
8:49	*Mesembryanthemum crystallinum* (Aizoaceae)	Crystalline Iceplant	Introduced		CA,AZ,BajaCA
8:50	*Calyptridium umbellatum* (Torrey) E. Greene (Portulacaceae)	Pussypaws	Native		c&nCA,BajaCA
9:5	*Lewisia cotyledon* (S. Watson) Robinson var. *howellii* (S. Watson) Jepson (Portulacaceae)	Howell's Lewisia	Native	CNPS Listed	nCA
9:9	*Silene hookeri* Nutt. (Caryophyllaceae)	Catchfly, Campion	Native		nCA
9:18	*Aquilegia formosa* Fischer (Ranunculaceae)	Columbine	Native		CA,BajaCA
9:26	*Delphinium parryi* A. Gray ssp. *parryi* (Ranunculaceae)	Parry's Larkspur	Native		c&sCA,BajaCA
9:29	*Ranunculus muricatus* L. (Ranunculaceae)	Butter Cup	Introduced		c&nCA
9:31	*Ranunculus* sp. (Ranunculaceae)	Butter Cup			
9:32	*Clematis lasiantha* Nutt. (Ranunculaceae)	Pipestems	Native		c&sCA,BajaCA
9:34	*Clematis pauciflora* Nutt. (Ranunculaceae)	Ropevine	Native		sCA,BajaCA
9:36	*Berberis nervosa* Pursh (Berberidaceae)	Oregon Grape, Barberry	Native		c&nCA
9:38	*Achlys triphylla* (Smith) D.C. ssp. *triphylla* (Berberidaceae)	Vanilla Leaf, Deer Foot	Native		nCA

Above left:
ACER GLABRUM VAR. TORREYI
(Mountain Maple, 13:31)

Above right:
ACER MACROPHYLLUM
(Big-Leaf Maple, 13:33)

Below left: HYPERICUM
CONCINNUM *(Gold Wire, 14:21)*

Below right:
MENTZELIA LAEVICAULIS
(Blazing Star, 14:34)

9:41	*Platystemon californicus* Benth. (Papaveraceae)	Cream Cups	Native	CNPS Listed	CA,AZ,BajaCA
9:42	*Papaver californicum* A. Gray (Papaveraceae)	Fire Poppy	Native		c&sCA,BajaCA
9:44	*Argemone munita* Durand & Hilg. (Papaveraceae)	Chicalote	Native		c&sCA,BajaCA
9:45	*Romneya coulteri* Harvey (Papaveraceae)	Coulter's Matilija Poppy	Native	CNPS Listed	sCA,BajaCA
9:46	*Romneya trichocalyx* Eastw. (Papaveraceae)	Hairy Matilija Poppy	Native		sCA,BajaCA
9:47	*Dendromecon rigida* Benth. (Papaveraceae)	Bush Poppy	Native		CA,BajaCA
9:48	*Eschscholzia californica* Cham. (Papaveraceae)	California Poppy	Native		CA,BajaCA
9:49	*Eschscholzia californica* Cham. (Papaveraceae)	California Poppy	Native		CA,BajaCA
9:50	*Isomeris arborea* Nutt. (Cappardaceae)	Bladderpod	Native		sCA,BajaCA
10:2	*Dicentra formosa* (Haw.) Walp. (Papaveraceae)	Oregon Bleeding Heart	Native		c&nCA
10:10	*Raphanus sativus* L. (Brassicaceae)	Wild Radish	Introduced		CA,BajaCA
10:11	*Brassica* sp. (Brassicaceae)	Mustard	Introduced		CA,BajaCA
10:12	*Brassica nigra* (L.) Koch (Brassicaceae)	Black Mustard	Introduced		CA,BajaCA
10:12	*Brassica rapa* L. (Brassicaceae)	Turnip, Field Mustard	Introduced		CA,BajaCA
10:16	*Cardamine* sp. (Brassicaceae)	Bitter Cress, Toothwort			
10:22	*Dithyrea californica* Harvey (Brassicaceae)	California Spectacle Pod	Native		c&sCA, AZ,BajaCA
10:23	*Lepidium fremontii* S. Watson var. *fremontii* (Brassicaceae)	Peppergrass, Pepperwort	Native		c&sCA,AZ
10:25	*Thysanocarpus curvipes* Hook. (Brassicaceae)	Lacepod, Fringepod	Native		CA,BajaCA
10:25	*Thysanocarpus radians* Benth. (Brassicaceae)	Lacepod, Fringepod	Native		CA
10:26	*Darlingtonia californica* Torrey (Sarraceniaceae)	California Pitcher Plant	Native	CNPS Listed	c&nCA
10:27	*Sedum spathulifolium* Hook. (Crassulaceae)		Native		CA
10:28	*Dudleya pulverulenta* (Nutt.) Britton & Rose ssp. *pulverulenta* (Crassulaceae)	Chalk Dudleya, Live-Forever	Native		c&sCA,AZ,BajaCA
10:31	*Dudleya cymosa* (Lemaire) Britton & Rose ssp. *cymosa* (Crassulaceae)		Native		c&nCA
10:38	*Heuchera sanguinea* Engelm. (Saxifragaceae)	Alumroot, Coral Bells	Introduced		CA
10:39	*Heuchera micrantha* Lindley (Saxifragaceae)	Alumroot	Native		c&nCA
10:43	*Carpenteria californica* Torrey (Philadelphaceae)	Tree-Anemone	Native	CNPS, CA Listed	cCA
10:50	*Ribes speciosum* Pursh (Grossulariaceae)	Fuchsia-Flowered Gooseberry	Native		c&sCA,BajaCA
11:1	*Ribes victoris* E. Greene (Grossulariaceae)	Victor's Gooseberry	Native	CNPS Listed	c&nCA
11:3	*Platanus racemosa* Nutt. (Platanaceae)	Western Sycamore	Native		CA,BajaCA
11:7	*Chamaebatia australis* (Brandegee) Abrams (Rosaceae)	Southern Mountain Misery	Native	CNPS Listed	sCA,BajaCA
11:8	*Rubus ursinus* Cham. & Schldl. (Rosaceae)	California Blackberry	Native		CA,BajaCA
11:9	*Rubus parviflorus* Nutt. (Rosaceae)	Thimbleberry	Native		CA
11:11	*Potentilla glandulosa* Lindley ssp. *nevadensis* (S.Watson) Keck (Rosaceae)	Cinquefoil	Native		CA
11:15	*Rosa californica* Cham. & Schldl. (Rosaceae)	California Rose	Native		CA,BajaCA
11:18	*Amelanchier utahensis* Koehne (Rosaceae)	Utah Service Berry	Native		CA,BajaCA
11:20	*Adenostoma fasciculatum* Hook. & Arn. (Rosaceae)	Chamise	Native		CA,BajaCA
11:24	*Prunus ilicifolia* (Nutt.) Walp. ssp. *ilicifolia* (Rosaceae)	Islay, Holly-Leaved Cherry	Native		sCA,BajaCA
11:25	*Prunus virginiana* L. var. *demissa* (Nutt.) Torrey (Rosaceae)	Western Choke-Cherry	Native		CA,nMex
11:27	*Prunus fremontii* S. Watson (Rosaceae)	Desert Apricot	Native		sCA,BajaCA
11:29	*Heteromeles arbutifolia* (Lindley) Roemer (Rosaceae)	Christmas Berry, Toyon	Native		CA,BajaCA
11:32	*Cercidium floridum* A. Gray ssp. *floridum* (Fabaceae)	Blue Palo Verde	Native		sCA,AZ,BajaCA
11:33	*Parkinsonia aculeata* L. (Fabaceae)	Mexican Palo Verde	Introduced		sCA,AZ,BajaCA
11:35	*Prosopis pubescens* Benth. (Fabaceae)	Screw Bean Mesquite, Tornillo	Native		sCA,AZ,BajaCA
11:36	*Acacia greggii* A. Gray (Fabaceae)	Catclaw	Native		c&sCA,BajaCA
11:41	*Lupinus nanus* Benth. (Fabaceae)	Lupine	Native		CA
11:43	*Lupinus albicaulis* Hook. (Fabaceae)	Lupine	Native		CA
11:45	*Lupinus bicolor* Lindley (Fabaceae)	Miniature Lupine	Native		CA,AZ,BajaCA
11:47	*Lupinus concinnus* J. Agardh (Fabaceae)	Bajada Lupine	Native		c&sCA,BajaCA
12:2	*Lupinus truncatus* Hook. & Arn. (Fabaceae)	Collar Lupine	Native		c&sCA,BajaCA
12:13	*Trifolium fucatum* Lindley (Fabaceae)	Bull Clover	Native		CA
12:22	*Lotus haydonii* (Orc.) E. Green (Fabaceae)	Haydon's Lotus, Pygmy Lotus	Native	CNPS Listed	sCA,BajaCA
12:29	*Hoita strobilina* (Hook. & Arn.) Rydb. (Fabaceae)	Loma Prieta Hoita	Native	CNPS Listed	cCA
12:33	*Psorothamnus schottii* (Torrey) Barneby (Fabaceae)	Indigo Bush	Native		sCA,AZ,BajaCA
12:38	*Astragalus lentiginosus* Hook. var. *borreganus* M.E. Jones (Fabaceae)	Borrego Milkvetch	Native	CNPS Listed	c&sCA,AZ,BajaCA
12:45	*Vicia americana* Willd. var. *americana* (Fabaceae)	American Vetch	Native		CA,BajaCA

12:48	*Lathyrus sulphureus* A. Gray (Fabaceae)	Wild Pea	Native		c&nCA
12:50	*Lathyrus vestitus* Nutt. (Fabaceae)	Wild Pea	Native		CA,BajaCA
13:1	*Lathyrus vestitus* Nutt. (Fabaceae)	Wild Pea	Native		CA,BajaCA
13:2	*Linum lewisii* Pursh (Linaceae)	Flax	Native		CA,AZ,BajaCA
13:3	*Oxalis oregana* Nutt. (Oxalidaceae)	Redwood Sorrel	Native		c&nCA
13:9	*Erodium moschatum* (L.) L'Hér (Geraniaceae)	Storksbill, Filaree	Introduced		CA,BajaCA
13:11	*Tetracoccus dioicus* C. Parry (Euphorbiaceae)	Parry's Tetracoccus	Native	CNPS Listed	sCA,BajaCA
13:16	*Chamaesyce polycarpa* (Benth.) Millsp. (Euphorbiaceae)	Prostrate Spurge	Native		c&sCA,BajaCA
13:18	*Euphorbia misera* Benth. (Euphorbiaceae)	Cliff Spurge	Native	CNPS Listed	sCA,BajaCA
13:20	*Larrea tridentata* (DC.) Cov. (Zygophyllaceae)	Creosote Bush	Native		c&sCA,AZ,BajaCA
13:25	*Toxicodendron diversilobum* (Torrey & A.Gray) E. Greene (Anacardiaceae)	Western Poison Oak	Native		CA,BajaCA
13:26	*Rhus integrifolia* (Nutt.) Brewer & S. Watson (Anacardiaceae)	Lemonadeberry	Native		sCA,BajaCA
13:31	*Acer glabrum* Pursh var. *torreyi* (E.Greene) F.J. Smiley (Aceraceae)	Mountain Maple	Native		nCA
13:33	*Acer macrophyllum* Pursh (Aceraceae)	Big-Leaf Maple	Native		CA
13:34	*Aesculus californica* (Spach.) Nutt. (Hippocastanaceae)	Buckeye, Horse Chestnut	Native		CA
13:45	*Ceanothus integerrimus* Hook. & Arn. (Rhamnaceae)	Deer Brush	Native		CA
13:47	*Ceanothus palmeri* Trel. (Rhamnaceae)	Palmer Ceanothus	Native		c&sCA BajaCA
13:48	*Ceanothus pinetorum* Cov. (Rhamnaceae)	Kern Ceanothus	Native	CNPS Listed	cCA
13:49	*Ceanothus prostratus* Benth. (Rhamnaceae)	Mahala Mat	Native		c&nCA
14:2	*Ceanothus cuneatus* (Hook.) Nutt. var. *rigidus* (Rhamnaceae)	Monterey Ceanothus	Native	CNPS Listed	c&sCA,BajaCA
14:3	*Ceanothus tomentosus* C. Parry (Rhamnaceae)	Ramona Lilac	Native		c&sCA,BajaCA
14:4	*Ceanothus tomentosus* C. Parry (Rhamnaceae)	Ramona Lilac	Native		c&sCA,BajaCA
14:8	*Lavatera assurgentiflora* Kellogg (Malvaceae)	Malva Rosa, Island Mallow	Native		c&sCA,BajaCA
14:11	*Sidalcea malvaeflora* (DC.) Benth. ssp. *sparsifolia* C. Hitchc. (Malvaceae)	Checker Mallow	Native		c&sCA,BajaCA
14:15	*Malacothamnus fasciculatus* (Torrey & A.Gray) E. Greene (Malvaceae)	Chaparral Mallow	Native		sCA,BajaCA
14:17	*Eremalche rotundifolia* (A. Gray) E. Greene (Malvaceae)	Desert Five-Spot	Native		c&sCA,AZ,BajaCA
14:21	*Hypericum concinnum* Benth. (Hypericaceae)	Gold-Wire	Native		c&nCA
14:25	*Fouquieria splendens* Engelm. ssp. *splendens* (Fouquieriaceae)	Ocotillo	Native		sCA,BajaCA
14:31	*Mentzelia lindleyi* Torrey & A. Gray (Loasaceae)	Lindley's Blazing Star	Native		CA
14:34	*Mentzelia laevicaulis* (Hook.) Torrey & A. Gray (Loasaceae)	Blazing Star	Native		CA
14:37	*Cylindropuntia bigelovii* (Engelm.) F.M. Knuth var. *bigelovii* (Cactaceae)	Teddy-Bear Cholla	Native		sCA,AZ,BajaCA
14:38	*Cylindropuntia echinocarpa* Engelm. & J. Bigelow (Cactaceae)	Silver or Golden Cholla	Native		c&sCA,AZ,BajaCA
14:39	*Cylindropuntia wolfii* (L.Benson) M.A. Baker (Cactaceae)	Wolf's Cholla	Native	CNPS Listed	sCA,BajaCA
14:40	*Cylindropuntia wolfii* (L.Benson) M.A .Baker (Cactaceae)	Wolf's Cholla	Native	CNPS Listed	sCA,BajaCA
14:41	*Cylindropuntia prolifera* (Engelm.) F.M. Knuth (Cactaceae)	Coast Cholla	Native		sCA,BajaCA
14:42	*Opuntia basilaris* Engelm. & J. Bigelow (Cactaceae)	Beavertail Cactus	Native		sCA,AZ,BajaCA
14:43	*Opuntia littoralis* (Engelm.) Cockerell (Cactaceae)	Coast Prickly-Pear	Native		sCA,BajaCA
14:44	*Opuntia dejecta* Salm-Dyck (Cactaceae)	Spiny Nopal	Introduced		sCA,BajaCA
14:46	*Bergerocactus emoryi* (Engelm.) Britton & Rose (Cactaceae)	Golden-Spined Cereus	Native	CNPS Listed	sCA,BajaCA
14:47	*Ferocactus cylindraceus* (Englem.) Orc. (Cactaceae)	California Barrel Cactus	Native		sCA,AZ,BajaCA
14:48	*Ferocactus viridescens* (Torrey & A.Gray) Britton & Rose (Cactaceae)	Coast Barrel Cactus	Native	CNPS Listed	sCA,BajaCA
14:48	*Mammillaria dioica* M.K. Brandegee (Cactaceae)	Fish-Hook Cactus	Native		sCA,BajaCA
14:49	*Cucurbita palmata* S. Watson (Cucurbitaceae)	Coyote Melon	Native		c&sCA,AZ,BajaCA
14:50	*Cucurbita foetidissima* Knuth (Cucurbitaceae)	Calabazilla	Native		c&sCA,BajaCA
15:1	*Marah macrocarpus* (E.Greene) E. Greene var. *macrocarpus* (Cucurbitaceae)	Manroot, Wild Cucumber	Native		sCA,BajaCA
15:15	*Clarkia amoena* (Lehm.) Nelson & J.F.Macbr. ssp. *amoena* (Onagraceae)	Godetia	Native		nCA
15:18	*Camissonia* sp. (Onagraceae)	Sun Cup			
15:20	*Camissonia cardiophylla* (Torrey) Raven var. *cardiophylla* (Onagraceae)	Evening Primrose	Native		c&sCA,AZ,BajaCA
15:24	*Camissonia ovata* (Torrey & A.Gray) Raven (Onagraceae)	Sun Cup	Native		c&nCA

Above left: Cylindropuntia wolfii *(Wolf's Cholla, 14:39)*

Above right: Cylindropuntia prolifera *(Coast Cholla, 14:41)*

Below left:
Nopalea sp. *(14:44)*

Below right:
Mammillaria dioica *(top) and* Ferocactus viridescens *(Coast Barrel Cactus, bottom, 14:48)*

Above left:
Marah macrocarpus var. macrocarpus *(15:01)*

Above right: Clarkia amoena ssp. amoena *(Godetia, 15:15)*

Below left: Oenothera deltoides ssp. cognata *(Basket Evening Primrose, 15:27)*

Below right: Eryngium aristulatum var. parishii *(San Diego Button Celery, 15:30)*

15:27	*Oenothera deltoides* Torrey & Frémont ssp. *cognata* (Jepson) Klein (Onagraceae)	Devil's Lantern, Basket Evening Primrose	Native		c&sCA,AZ,BajaCA
15:30	*Eryngium aristulatum* Jepson var. *parishii* (J.Coulter & Rose) Jepson (Apiaceae)	San Diego Button Celery	Native	CNPS, CA/FE Listed	sCA,BajaCA
15:41	*Foeniculum vulgare* Miller (Apiaceae)	Fennel	Introduced		CA,BajaCA
15:43	*Lomatium lucidum* (Torrey & A.Gray) Jepson (Apiaceae)	Shiny Lomatium	Native		c&sCA,BajaCA
15:46	*Heracleum lanatum* Michaux (Apiaceae)	Cow Parsnip	Native		CA
15:47	*Cornus sericea* L. ssp. *sericea* (Cornaceae)	American Dogwood	Native		CA,Mex
15:49	*Cornus nuttallii* Audubon (Cornaceae)	Mountain Dogwood	Native		CA
16:3	*Sarcodes sanguinea* Torrey (Ericaceae)	Snow Plant	Native		CA,BajaCA
16:5	*Rhododendron occidentale* (Torrey & A.Gray) A. Gray (Ericaceae)	Western Azalea	Native		CA
16:6	*Rhododendron macrophyllum* D. Don (Ericaceae)	California Rose-Bay	Native		c&nCA
16:14	*Arctostaphylos pungens* Kunth (Ericaceae)	Manzanita	Native		c&sCA,BajaCA
16:16	*Xylococcus bicolor* Nutt. (Ericaceae)	Coast Manzanita, Mission Manzanita	Native		sCA,BajaCA
16:18	*Dodecatheon clevelandii* E. Greene ssp. *sanctarum* (E.Greene) Abrams (Primulaceae)	Shooting Star	Native		sCA,BajaCA
16:21	*Armeria maritima* (Miller) Willd. ssp. *californica* (Boiss.) A.A. Heller (Plumbaginaceae)	Sea Pink, Thrift	Native		CA
16:22	*Styrax officinalis* L. var. *redivivus* (Torrey) H. Howard (Styracaceae)	Snowdrop Bush	Native		CA
16:25	*Gentiana calycosa* Griseb. (Gentianaceae)	Gentian	Native		c&nCA
16:34	*Asclepias eriocarpa* Benth. (Asclepiadaceae)	Indian Milkweed, Kotolo	Native		CA,BajaCA
16:38	*Calystegia* sp. (Convolvulaceae)	Morning Glory			
17:11	*Linanthus grandiflorus* (Benth.) E. Greene (Polemoniaceae)	Large-Flowered Linanthus	Native	CNPS Listed	n&cCA
17:13	*Linanthus floribundus* (A.Gray) Milliken ssp. *floribundus* (Polemoniaceae)	Many-Flowered Linanthus	Native		c&sCA,BajaCA
17:18	*Hydrophyllum occidentale* (S.Watson) A. Gray (Hydrophyllaceae)	Western Waterleaf	Native		c&nCA
17:20	*Nemophila menziesii* Hook. & Arn. var. *atomaria* (Fischer & C.Meyer) Chandler (Hydrophyllaceae)	Baby Blue-Eyes	Native		c&nCA
17:30	*Phacelia grandiflora* (Benth.) A. Gray (Hydrophyllaceae)	Large-Flowered Phacelia	Native		sCA,BajaCA
17:36	*Eriodictyon tomentosum* Benth. (Hydrophyllaceae)	Yerba Santa	Native		cCA
17:40	*Cynoglossum grande* Lehm. (Boraginaceae)	Hound's Tongue	Native		CA
17:46	*Cryptantha racemosa* (S.Watson) E. Greene (Boraginaceae)	Woody Cryptantha	Native		c&sCA AZ,BajaCA
18:7	*Trichostema lanatum* Benth. (Lamiaceae)	Woolly Bluecurls	Native		c&sCA,BajaCA
18:9	*Salazaria mexicana* Torrey (Lamiaceae)	Bladder Sage	Native		c&sCA,BajaCA
18:11	*Prunella vulgaris* L. var. *lanceolata* (Barton) Fern. (Lamiaceae)	Self-Heal	Native		sCA,BajaCA
18:13	*Salvia mellifera* E. Greene (Lamiaceae)	Black Sage	Native		c&sCA,BajaCA
18:14	*Salvia apiana* Jepson (Lamiaceae)	White Sage	Native		sCA,BajaCA
18:15	*Salvia carduacea* Benth. (Lamiaceae)	Thistle Sage	Native		c&sCA,BajaCA
18:16	*Salvia clevelandii* (A.Gray) E. Greene (Lamiaceae)	Cleveland Sage, Fragrant Sage	Native		sCA,BajaCA
18:17	*Salvia columbariae* Benth. (Lamiaceae)	Chia	Native		CA,AZ,BajaCA
18:18	*Salvia dorrii* (Kellogg) Abrams var. *incana* (A.Gray) J.L. Strachan (Lamiaceae)	Fleshy Sage	Native	CNPS Listed	nCA
18:19	*Melissa officinalis* L. (Lamiaceae)	Bee Balm	Introduced		c&nCA
18:20	*Satureja douglasii* (Benth.) Briq. (Lamiaceae)	Yerba Buena	Native		CA
18:27	*Monardella macrantha* A. Gray ssp. *macrantha* (Lamiaceae)	Scarlet Monardella	Native		sCA,BajaCA
18:30	*Datura wrightii* Regel (Solanaceae)	Jimson Weed, Thorn Apple	Introduced		CA,BajaCA
18:35	*Nicotiana glauca* Graham (Solanaceae)	Tree Tobacco	Introduced		CA,BajaCA
19:5	*Penstemon rostriflorus* Kellogg (Scrophulariaceae)	Beardtongue	Native		c&sCA,AZ,BajaCA
19:7	*Penstemon centranthifolius* (Benth.) Benth. (Scrophulariaceae)	Scarlet Bugler	Native		CA,BajaCA
19:7	*Penstemon labrosus* (A. Gray) Hook.f. (Scrophulariaceae)	Beardtongue	Native		sCA,BajaCA
19:9	*Keckiella cordifolia* (Benth.) Straw (Scrophulariaceae)	Climbing Bush Penstemon	Native		sCA,BajaCA
19:11	*Penstemon heterophyllus* Lindley var. *heterophyllus* (Scrophulariaceae)	Foothill Penstemon	Native		CA
19:12	*Penstemon grinnellii* Eastw. var. *grinnellii* (Scrophulariaceae)	Beardtongue	Native		sCA,BajaCA

Above left: FOENICULUM VULGARE *(Fennel, 15:41)*
Fennel is a non-native, invasive perennial herb, conspicuous along roadsides, streambeds, and wasteplaces. The plants, which are members of the Carrot family, grow up to 6 feet tall, and have a distinctive odor of anise or licorice. Native to Europe and the Mediterranean area, Fennel has been used for culinary and medicinal purposes for centuries and has become naturalized around the world. Tolerating dry, sandy, acidic soils, it can reproduce both by seed and from the crown or root system, so it is very successful at spreading. Though not native itself, Fennel has become a common host plant for the larvae of a native butterfly, the Anise Swallowtail.

Above right:
CORNUS SERICEA SSP. SERICEA *(American Dogwood, 15:47)*

Below: CAMISSONIA SP. *(Sun Cup, 15:18)*

19:13	*Penstemon laetus* A. Gray var. *laetus* (Scrophulariaceae)	Beardtongue	Native	CA
19:15	*Penstemon spectabilis* Thurber (Scrophulariaceae)	Showy Penstemon	Native	sCA,BajaCA
19:20	*Mimulus aurantiacus* Curtis (Scrophulariaceae)	Coast Monkey Flower	Native	CA,BajaCA
19:23	*Mimulus guttatus* DC. (Scrophulariaceae)	Seep Monkey Flower	Native	CA,BajaCA
19:28	*Castilleja foliolosa* Hook. & Arn. (Scrophulariaceae)	Woolly Indian Paintbrush	Native	CA,BajaCA
19:29	*Castilleja linariifolia* Benth. (Scrophulariaceae)	Indian Paintbrush, Owl's Clover	Native	CA
19:31	*Castilleja parviflora* Bong. (Scrophulariaceae)	Indian Paintbrush, Owl's Clover	Native	c&nCA
19:37	*Chilopsis linearis* (Cav.) Sweet ssp. *arcuata* (Fosb.) Henrickson (Bignoniaceae)	Desert Willow	Native	sCA,BajaCA
19:44	*Sambucus mexicana* C. Presl (Caprifoliaceae)	Blue Elderberry	Native	CA,BajaCA
19:48	*Dipsacus sativus* (L.) Honck. (Dipsacaceae)	Fuller's Teasel	Introduced	CA
20:7	*Cichorium intybus* L. (Asteraceae)	Chicory	Introduced	CA,BajaCA
20:13	*Rafinesquia neomexicana* A. Gray (Asteraceae)	Desert Chicory	Native	c&sCA,BajaCA
20:18	*Malacothrix californica* DC. (Asteraceae)	Desert Dandelion	Native	c&sCA,BajaCA
20:19	*Malacothrix floccifera* (DC.) Blake (Asteraceae)		Native	CA
20:22	*Agoseris grandiflora* (Nutt.) E. Greene (Asteraceae)	Large-Flowered Agoseris	Native	CA
20:27	*Acourtia microcephala* DC. (Asteraceae)		Native	sCA,BajaCA
20:43	*Solidago californica* Nutt. (Asteraceae)	California Goldenrod	Native	CA,BajaCA
21:3	*Xylorhiza tortifolia* (Torrey & A.Gray) E. Greene var. *tortifolia* (Asteraceae)	Mohave Aster	Native	c&sCA,AZ
21:4	*Erigeron peregrinus* (Pursh) E. Greene var. *callianthemus* (E.Greene) Conq. (Asteraceae)	Fleabane Daisy	Native	c&nCA
21:6	*Erigeron glaucus* Ker-Gawler (Asteraceae)	Seaside Daisy	Native	CA
21:25	*Viguiera laciniata* A. Gray (Asteraceae)	San Diego Sunflower	Native — CNPS Listed	sCA,BajaCA
21:28	*Balsamorhiza deltoidea* Nutt. (Asteraceae)	Balsam Root	Native	CA
21:30	*Wyethia angustifolia* (DC.) Nutt. (Asteraceae)	Mules Ears	Native	c&nCA
21:33	*Encelia farinosa* Torrey & A. Gray (Asteraceae)	Brittlebush, Incienso	Native	sCA,AZ,BajaCA
21:38	*Coreopsis maritima* (Nutt.) Hook. (Asteraceae)	Sea Dahlia	Native — CNPS Listed	sCA,BajaCA
21:41	*Coreopsis* sp. (Asteraceae)			
22:1	*Layia platyglossa* (Fischer & C.Meyer) A. Gray (Asteraceae)	Tidy Tips	Native	CA,BajaCA
22:23	*Chamomilla suaveolens* (Pursh) Rydb. (Asteraceae)	Pineapple Weed, Rayless Chamomile	Native	sCA,BajaCA
22:34	*Cirsium occidentale* (Nutt.) Jepson var. *californicum* (A.Gray) Keil & C. Turner (Asteraceae)	California Thistle	Native	c&sCA,BajaCA
22:36	*Cirsium occidentale* (Nutt.) Jepson (Asteraceae)	Cobwebby Thistle	Native — CNPS Listed	cCA,BajaCA
22:39	*Agoseris* sp. (Asteraceae)			

Above left: ARMERIA
MARITIMA SSP. CALIFORNICA
(Sea Pink, 16:21)

Above right: STYRAX
OFFICINALIS VAR. REDIVIVUS
(Snowdrop Bush, 16:22)

Below: CALYSTEGIA SP.
(Morning Glory, 16:38)

Above left: Gentiana calycosa *(16:25)*

Above right: Eriastrum densifolium *(17:11)*

Below left: Linanthus floribundus ssp. floribundus *(17:13)*

Below right: Hydrophyllum occidentale *(17:18)*

Above left: ERIODICTYON TOMENTOSUM *(17:36)*

Above right: TRICHOSTEMA LANATUM *(Woolly Bluecurls, 18:07)*

Below left: SALAZARIA MEXICANA *(Bladder Sage, 18:09)*

Below right: SALVIA APIANA *(White Sage, 18:14)*

Above left: Salvia dorrii var. incana *(Fleshy Sage, 18:18)*

Above right: Salvia carduacea *(Thistle Sage, 18:15)*

Below left: Salvia clevelandii *(Cleveland Sage, 18:16)*

Below right: Salvia columbariae *(Chia, 18:17)*

Above left: Prunella
vulgaris var. lanceolata
(18:11)

Above right: Monardella
macrantha ssp. macrantha
(18:27)

Below left: Datura wrightii
(Jimson Weed, 18:30)

Below right: Castilleja
parviflora *(19:31)*

Above left: PENSTEMON ROSTRIFLORUS *(19:05)*

Above right: PENSTEMON CENTRANTHIFOLIUS *(Scarlet Bugler, right) and* PENSTEMON LABROSUS *(left, 19:07)*

Below left: PENSTEMON LAETUS VAR. LAETUS *(19:13)*

Below right: PENSTEMON SPECTABILIS VAR. SPECTABILIS *(Showy Penstemon, 19:15)*

Above left: Dipsacus sativus
(Fuller's Teasel, 19:48)

Above right:
Rafinesquia neomexicana
(Desert Chicory, 20:13)

Below left: Xylorhiza
tortifolia var. tortifolia
(Mohave Aster, 21:03)

Below right:
Erigeron peregrinus
var. callianthemus *(21:04)*

Above left: Malacothrix californica *(20:18)*

Above right: Malacothrix floccifera *(20:19)*

Below left: Acourtia microcephala *(20:27)*

Below right: Chamomilla suaveolens *(Pineapple Weed, 22:23)*

Above left: Wyethia
angustifolia *(21:30)*

Above right: Balsamorhiza
deltoidea *(Balsam Root, 21:28)*

Below left: Agoseris
grandiflora *(20:22)*

Below right: Agoseris sp.
(22:39)

Index

Italic type indicates illustration pages.

A

Abronia maritima, 126, 187
Abronia umbellata ssp. *breviflora*, 126, 187
Acacia greggii, 179, 189
Acer glabrum var. *torreyi*, 188, 190
Acer macrophyllum, 188, 190
Achlys triphylla ssp. *triphylla*, 90, 187
Acourtia microcephala, 195, 203
Adenostoma fasciculatum, 12, 189
Adiantum aleuticum, 13, 182
Adobe Lily, 39, 182
Aesculus californica, 14, 190
Agave deserti, 129, 187
Agoseris grandiflora, 195, 204
Agoseris sp., 195, 204
Alamo Cottonwood, 147, 187
Allium peninsulare var. *peninsulare*, 83, 185
Allium praecox, 158, 185
Alum Root, 97, 189
Amelanchier utahensis, 177, 189
American Dogwood, 193, 194
American Vetch, 183, 189
Anemone occidentalis, 80, 182
Anemopsis californica, 15, 187
Annual Bluegrass, 145, 185
Aquilegia formosa, 87, 187
Arctostaphylos pungens, 35, 193
Argemone munita, 119, 189
Armeria maritima ssp. *californica*, 193, 196
Arroyo Willow, 87, 187
Asarum caudatum, 16, 187
Asclepias eriocarpa, 133, 193
Astragalus lentiginosus var. *borreganus*, 183, 189
Atriplex hymenelytra, 123, 187
Azalea, Western, 152, 193

B

Baby Blue-Eyes, 4, 127, 182, 193
Bajada Lupine, 178, 189
Balsam Root, 17, 195, 204
Balsamorhiza deltoidea, 17, 195, 204
Barrel Cactus, California, 74, 128, 190
Basket Evening Primrose, 192, 193
Beardtongue, 140, 193, 195
Beargrass, 169, 185
Beavertail Cactus, 137, 190
Bee Balm, 159, 193
Berberis nervosa, 18, 187
Bergerocactus emoryi, 19, 128, 190
Big-Leaf Maple, 188, 190
biological diversity
    decline of, 154
    importance of, 153–60
    of Southern California, 113–35
    preserving, 159
    San Diego County as "hot spot" of, 117
Bischoff, Franz A., 87, 90, 92
    Roses, 89
    Untitled still life, 89
Bitter Root, 154, 182
Black Oak, California, 2, 149, 150, 187
Black Sage, 159, 193
Blackberry, California, 130, 189
Bladder Sage, 193, 198
Bladderpod, 174, 189
Blazing Star, 188, 190
Blue Dicks, 36, 185
Blue Elderberry, 166, 195
Blue Flag, Western, 98, 187
Blue Palo Verde, 177, 189
Borglum, Elizabeth Putnam, 79, 82
Borglum, John Gutzon, 79, 82
Borrego Milkvetch, 183, 189
botanical illustration, 38
    as decoration for pottery, 32
Brassica sp., 136, 174, 189
Bristly Langloisia, 124, 182
Brittlebush, 132, 195
Brodiaea minor, 83, 185

Brodiaea purdyi, 90, 185
Bromus madritensis ssp. *rubens*, 80, 185
Brown, Benjamin C., 87
Buckeye, California, 14, 190
Buckwheat, California, 128, 187
Buffalo Squash, 63, 190
Bush Poppy, 115, 189
Butter-and-Eggs, 46, 182
Buttercup, 53, 78, 122, 187

C
Calabazilla, 63, 190
California Barrel Cactus, 74, 128, 190
California Black Oak, 2, 149, 150, 187
California Blackberry, 130, 189
California Buckeye, 14, 190
California Buckwheat, 128, 187
California Cord Grass, 124, 185
California Evening Primrose, 91, 182
California Fawn Lily, 79, 185
California Goldenrod, 83, 195
California Lady's Slipper, 38, 187
California Pitcher Plant, 11, 68, 189
California Polypody, 146, 182
California Poppy, 73, 121, 189
California Rose-Bay, 86, 193
California Sandwort, 45, 111, 182
California Thistle, 58, 195
California Wild Rose, 1, 164, 189
Calochortus amabilis, 20, 185
Calochortus concolor, 118, 185
Calochortus pulchellus, 49, 185
Calochortus splendens, 21, 42, 185
Calochortus tolmiei, 133, 182
Calochortus uniflorus, 130, 182
Calochortus venustus,
    22, 23, 24, 42, 43, 173, 185
Calochortus vestae, 42, 185
Calypso bulbosa, 38, 182
Calyptridium umbellatum, 115, 187
Calystegia sp., 193, 196
Camissonia ovata, 81, 190
Camissonia sp., 190, 194
Canyon Live Oak, 148, 187
Cardamine sp., 25, 189
Carex scopulorum var. *bracteosa*, 79, 185
Carpenteria californica, 26, 189
Castilleja exserta ssp. *exserta*, 136, 182

Castilleja foliolosa, 80, 195
Castilleja parviflora, 195, 200
Castilleja subinclusa ssp. *subinclusa*, 156
Catclaw, 179, 189
Ceanothus cuneatus var. *rigidus*, 186, 190
Ceanothus integerrimus, 186, 190
Ceanothus palmeri, 35, 190
Ceanothus pinetorum, 186, 190
Ceanothus prostratus, 27, 190
Ceanothus tomentosus, 28, 186, 190
Celtis reticulata, 174, 187
Cephalanthera austinae, 154, 182
Cercidium floridum ssp. *floridum*, 177, 189
Chain Fern, Giant, 45, 182
Chalk Dudleya, 70, 189
Chamaebatia australis, 176, 189
Chamaesyce polycarpa, 135, 190
Chamise, 12, 189
Chamomilla suaveolens, 195, 203
Chaparral Mallow, 108, 190
Checker Mallow, 184, 190
Cheilanthes newberryi, 123, 182
Chia, 193, 199
Chicalote, 119, 189
Chicory, 154, 195
Chilopsis linearis, 57, 195
Chocolate Lily, 36, 187
Choke-Cherry, Western, 177, 189
Christmas Berry, 96, 189
Cichorium intybus, 154, 195
Cincinnati Art Museum
    collection of Valentien paintings, 51, 75
Cirsium occidentale, 58, 59, 195
Cirsium occidentale var. *californicum*, 58, 195
Clarkia amoena ssp. *amoena*, 190, 192
Clematis lasiantha, 82, 187
Clematis pauciflora, 60, 187
Cleveland Sage, 193, 199
Cliff Spurge, 127, 190
Climbing Bush Penstemon, 157, 193
Coast Barrel Cactus, 190, 191
Coast Cholla, 190, 191
Coast Manzanita, 170, 193
Coast Monkey Flower, 133, 195
Coast Prickly Pear, 121, 190, *back cover*
Coast Range Melic, 41, 185
Coast Redwood, 168, 185
Coastal Fawn Lily, 80, 182
Coastal Wood Fern, 53, 182

Coffee Fern, *119*, *182*
Columbine, Western, *87*, *187*
Common Velvet Grass, *78*, *185*
Cord Grass, California, *124*, *185*
Coreopsis maritima, *118*, *195*
Coreopsis sp., *61*, *195*
Cornus nuttallii, *62*, *193*
Cornus sericea ssp. *sericea*, *193*, *194*
Cotton Fern, *123*, *182*
Cow Parsnip, *94*, *193*
Coyote Melon, *131*, *190*
Cream Cups, *91*, *189*
Creosote Bush, *132*, *190*
Cryptantha racemosa, *155*, *193*
Crystalline Iceplant, *110*, *187*
Cucurbita foetidissima, *63*, *190*
Cucurbita palmata, *131*, *190*
Cupressus macrocarpa, *126*, *185*
Cylindropuntia bigelovii var. *bigelovii*, *64*, *190*
Cylindropuntia prolifera, *190*, *191*
Cylindropuntia wolfii, *65*, *190*, *191*
Cynoglossum grande, *66*, *193*
Cyperus virens, *172*, *185*
Cypripedium californicum, *38*, *187*
Cypripedium montanum, *67*, *187*

D

Darlingtonia californica, *11*, *68*, *189*
Datura wrightii, *193*, *200*
de Longpré, Paul. *See* Longpré, Paul de
Death Camas, *171*, *185*
Deer Brush, *186*, *190*
Delphinium depauperatum, *81*, *182*
Delphinium parryi ssp. *parryi*, *81*, *187*
Dendromecon rigida, *115*, *189*
Desert Agave, *129*, *187*
Desert Apricot, *131*, *189*
Desert Chicory, *195*, *202*
Desert Five-Spot, *72*, *190*
Desert Holly, *123*, *187*
Desert Lily, *95*, *185*
Desert Star, *124*, *182*
Desert Trumpet, *125*, *187*
Desert Willow, *57*, *195*
Dicentra formosa, *174*, *189*
Dichelostemma capitatum, *36*, *185*
Diogenes' Lantern, *20*, *185*
Dipsacus sativus, *195*, *202*
Distichlis spicata, *40*, *185*

Dithyrea californica, *175*, *189*
Dodecatheon clevelandii, *69*, *193*
Dodecatheon hendersonii, *39*, *182*
Douglas' Meadowfoam, *130*, *182*
Douglas' Monkey Flower, *46*, *182*
Dryopteris arguta, *53*, *182*
Dudleya cymosa ssp. *cymosa*, *175*, *189*
Dudleya pulverulenta, *70*, *189*
Duveneck, Frank, *29*, *31*
Dwarf Brodiaea, *83*, *185*
Dwarf Larkspur, *81*, *182*

E

Early Onion, *158*, *185*
Encelia farinosa, *132*, *195*
Equisetum telmateia, *71*, *182*
Eremalche rotundifolia, *72*, *190*
Eriastrum densifolium, *197*
Erigeron glaucus, *86*, *195*
Erigeron peregrinus var. *callianthemus*, *195*, *202*
Eriodictyon tomentosum, *193*, *198*
Eriogonum fasciculatum, *128*, *187*
Eriogonum inflatum, *125*, *187*
Eriogonum thurberi, *120*, *187*
Eriogonum vimineum, *114*, *187*
Eriophyllum pringlei, *46*, *182*
Eriophyllum wallacei, *46*, *182*
Erodium macrophyllum, *127*, *182*
Erodium moschatum, *184*, *190*
Eryngium aristulatum var. *parishii*, *192*, *193*
Erythronium californicum, *79*, *185*
Erythronium grandiflorum, *49*, *79*, *185*
Erythronium hendersonii, *79*, *187*
Erythronium oregonum, *79*, *187*
Erythronium revolutum, *80*, *182*
Eschscholzia californica, *73*, *121*, *189*
Euphorbia misera, *127*, *190*
Evening Primrose, *121*, *190*
Evening Primrose, California, *91*, *182*
Evening Snow, *81*, *182*

F

Fairy Slipper, *38*, *182*
Fawn Lily, California, *79*, *185*
Fennel, *193*, *194*
Ferocactus cylindraceus, *74*, *190*
Ferocactus viridescens, *190*, *191*
Filaree, *184*, *190*

Fire Poppy, *39*, 189
Five-Finger Maidenhair Fern, *13*, 182
Fivespot, *46*, 182
Flax, *104*, 190
Fleshy Sage, *193*, *199*
Foeniculum vulgare, *193*, *194*
Foothill Penstemon, *140*, 193
Fouquieria splendens, *3, 93*, 190
Four O'Clock, Giant, *114*, 187
Foxtail Chess, *80*, 185
Fragaria vesca, *131*, 182
Francisco, John Bond, 79, 82
Fremont Cottonwood, *147*, 187
Fringed Checker Mallow, *125*, 182
Fritillaria biflora, *36*, 187
Fritillaria pluriflora, *39*, 182
Fuchsia-Flowered Gooseberry, *176*, 189
Fuller's Teasel, *195*, *202*

G
Gamble, John, 92
Gentiana calycosa, *193*, *197*
Ghost Flower, *91*, 182
Giant Chain Fern, *45*, 182
Giant Four O'Clock, *114*, 187
Giant Horsetail, *71*, 182
Glacier Lily, *49, 79*, 185
Glyptopleura marginata, *46*, 182
Godetia, *190*, *192*
Gold Wire, *188*, *190*
Goldback Fern, *53*, *182*
Golden-Bowl Mariposa Lily, *118*, 185
Goldenrod, California, *83*, 195

H
Hairy Matilija Poppy, *6, 163*, 189, *front cover*
Haydon's Lotus, *127*, 189
Heart's Ease, Western, *133*, 182
Henderson's Fawn Lily, *79*, 187
Henderson's Triteleia, *173*, 185
Heracleum lanatum, *94*, 193
Hesperocallis undulata, *95*, 185
Hesperostipa comata ssp. *intermedia*, *122*, 185
Hesperoyucca whipplei, *117*, 187
Heteromeles arbutifolia, *8, 96*, 189
Heuchera micrantha, *176*, 189
Heuchera sanguinea, *97*, 189
Hill Lotus, *131*, 182
Hoita strobilina, *127*, 189

Holcus lanatus, *78*, 185
Holly-Leaved Cherry, *130*, 189
Hooker's Silene, *54*, 187
Horsetail, Giant, *71*, 182
Hound's Tongue, *66*, 193
Howell's Lewisia, *100*, 187
Hydrophyllum occidentale, *193*, *197*
Hypericum concinnum, *188*, *190*

I
Incienso, *132*, 195
Indian Milkweed, *133*, 193
Indigo Bush, *180*, 189
Iris, *82*, 187
Iris macrosiphon, *82*, 187
Iris missouriensis, *98*, 187
Island Mallow, *48*, 190
Isomeris arborea, *174*, 189

J
Jimson Weed, *193*, *200*
Johnsongrass, *80*, 185
Joshua Tree, *129*, 187
Judson, William Lees, 87

K
Keckiella cordifolia, *157*, 193
Keith, William, 79
Kern Ceanothus, *186*, *190*
Knobcone Pine, *117*, 185
Kotolo, *133*, 193

L
Lady's Slipper, California, *38*, 187
Lamarckia aurea, *53*, 185
Langloisia setosissima ssp. *setosissima*, *124*, 182
Large-Flowered Star Tulip, *130*, 182
Larrea tridentata, *121, 132*, 190
Lathyrus sulphureus, *183*, *190*
Lathyrus vestitus, *99, 183*, 190
Lavatera assurgentiflora, *48*, 190
Layia platyglossa, *155*, 195
Lemon Lily, *49*, 187
Lemonadeberry, *161*, 190
Lepidium fremontii var. *fremontii*, *175*, 189
Lewisia cotyledon var. *howellii*, *100*, 187
Lewisia rediviva, *154*, 182
Lilium humboldtii ssp. *ocellatum*, *101*, 187

Lilium parryi, 49, 187
Lilium rubescens, 102, 187
Lilium washingtonianum, 103, 187
Limnanthes douglasii ssp. *douglasii*, 130, 182
Linanthus dichotomus, 81, 182
Linanthus floribundus ssp. *floribundus*, 193, 197
Lindley's Blazing Star, 109, 190
Linum lewisii, 104, 190
Lithocarpus densiflorus, 116, 187
Loma Prieta Hoita, 127, 189
Lomatium lucidum, 156, 193
Longpré, Paul de, 83, 86, 92
    botanical illustration of, 86
    Fresh from the Garden, 88
    Papa Gontier Roses, 88
    Roses, 85
    Violets, 84
    White and Yellow Mums, 84
    Wild Roses with Bee, 85
Long-rayed Triteleia, 172, 185
Longtongue, 41, 185
Lotus haydonii, 127, 189
Lotus humistratus, 131, 182
Lupine, Miniature, 107, 189
Lupinus albicaulis, 178, 189
Lupinus bicolor, 107, 189
Lupinus concinnus, 178, 189
Lupinus nanus, 106, 189
Lupinus truncatus, 179, 189
Lysichiton americanum, 105, 185

M

Mahala Mat, 27, 190
Malacothamnus fasciculatus, 108, 190
Malacothrix californica, 195, 203
Malacothrix floccifera, 195, 203
Mammillaria dioica, 190, 191
Manzanita, 35
Marah macrocarpus var. *macrocarpus*, 190, 192
Mariposa Lily, 22–24, 42, 43, 185
Matilija Poppy, 77, 162, 189
Matilija Poppy, Hairy, 6, 163, 189, *front cover*
Maul Oak, 148, 187
Melica imperfecta, 41, 185
Melissa officinalis, 159, 193
Mentzelia laevicaulis, 188, 190
Mentzelia lindleyi, 109, 190
Mersfelder, Jules, 79

Mesembryanthemum crystallinum, 110, 187
Mexican Palo Verde, 178, 189
Mimulus aurantiacus, 133, 195
Mimulus douglasii, 46, 182
Mimulus guttatus, 133, 195
Miniature Lupine, 107, 189
Minuartia californica, 45, 111, 182
Mirabilis multiflora var. *pubescens*, 114, 187
Mission Manzanita, 170, 193
Mohave Aster, 195, 202
Mohavea confertiflora, 91, 182
Monardella macrantha ssp. *macrantha*, 193, 200
Monoptilon belliodes, 124, 182
Monterey Ceanothus, 186, 190
Monterey Cypress, 126, 185
Monterey Pine, 143, 185
Morning Glory, 193, 196
Mosquito Bills, 39, 182
Mount Diablo Fairy Lantern, 49, 185
Mountain Dogwood, 62, 193
Mountain Lady's Slipper, 67, 187
Mountain Maple, 188, 190
Mustard, 136, 174, 189
Mutton Grass, 41, 185

N

Nassella pulchra, 112, 185
Natal Grass, 136, 185
Needle and Thread, 122, 185
Nemophila maculata, 46, 182
Nemophila menziesii var. *atomaria*, 4, 193
Nemophila menziesii var. *menziesii*, 127, 182
Net-Leaf Hackberry, 174, 187
Nicotiana glauca, 136, 193
Nopalea sp., 191
Nuttall's Scrub Oak, 116, 187

O

Ocellated Humboldt Lily, 101, 187
Ocotillo, 3, 93, 190
Oenothera californica ssp. *californica*, 91, 182
Oenothera deltoides ssp. *cognata*, 192, 193
Opuntia basilaris, 137, 190
Opuntia littoralis, 121, 190, *back cover*
Oregon Bleeding Heart, 174, 189
Oregon Fawn Lily, 79, 187
Oregon Grape, 18, 187
Our Lord's Candle, 117, 187
Oxalis oregana, 184, 190

P

Panicum capillare, 138, 185
Papaver californicum, 39, 189
Parkinsonia aculeata, 178, 189
Parry's Larkspur, 81, 187
Parry's Tetracoccus, 48, 190
Pasque Flower, 80, 182
Pellaea andromedifolia, 119, 182
Penstemon centranthifolius, 193, 201
Penstemon grinnellii var. *grinnellii*, 139, 193
Penstemon heterophyllus, 140, 193
Penstemon labrosus, 193, 201
Penstemon laetus var. *laetus*, 195, 201
Penstemon rostriflorus, 193, 201
Penstemon spectabilis, 195, 201
Pentagramma triangularis ssp. *triangularis*, 53, 182
Pepper Tree, 34
Phacelia grandiflora, 141, 193
Phantom Orchid, 154, 182
Pineapple Weed, 195, 203
Pink Sand Verbena, 126, 187
Pinus attenuata, 117, 185
Pinus monticola, 172, 185
Pinus ponderosa, 142, 182
Pinus radiata, 143, 185
Pinus torreyana, 134, 185
Pipestems, 82, 187
Pitcher Plant, California, 11, 68, 189
Platanthera leucostachys, 123, 187
Platanus racemosa, 144, 189
Platystemon californicus, 91, 189
Poa annua, 145, 185
Poa fendleriana ssp. *longiligula*, 41, 185
Poison Oak, Western, 40, 190
Polypodium californicum, 146, 182
Polypody, California, 146, 182
Polystichum munitum, 45, 182
Ponderosa Pine, 142, 182
Poppy, California, 73, 121, 189
Populus fremontii, 147, 187
Potentilla glandulosa ssp. *nevadensis*, 177, 189
Prosopis pubescens, 128, 189
Prunella vulgaris var. *lanceolata*, 193, 200
Prunus fremontii, 131, 189
Prunus ilicifolia ssp. *ilicifolia*, 130, 189
Prunus virginiana var. *demissa*, 177, 189
Psorothamnus schottii, 180, 189

Purple Mouse Ears, 46, 182
Purple Needlegrass, 112, 185
Purple Owl's Clover, 136, 182
Pussy Ears, 133, 182
Pussy Paws, 115, 187
Pygmy Lotus, 127, 189
Pyrola picta, 154, 182

Q

Quercus chrysolepis, 148, 187
Quercus dumosa, 116, 187
Quercus kelloggii, 2, 149, 150, 187
Quercus lobata, 151, 187

R

Rafinesquia neomexicana, 195, 202
Ranunculus muricatus, 78, 187
Ranunculus sp., 53, 122, 187
Raphanus sativus, 158, 189
Red Brome, 80, 185
Red Sand Verbena, 126, 187
Red-flowered Onion, 83, 185
Redmond, Granville, 92
Redwood Lily, 102, 187
Redwood Sorrel, 184, 190
Redwood, Coast, 168, 185
Rhododendron macrophyllum, 86, 193
Rhododendron occidentale, 152, 193
Rhus integrifolia, 161, 190
Rhynchelytrum repens, 136, 185
Ribes speciosum, 176, 189
Ribes victoris, 176, 189
Rix, Julian, 79
Roble, 151, 187
Romneya coulteri, 77, 162, 189
Romneya trichocalyx, 6, 163, 189, *front cover*
Rookwood Pottery, 29–33, 75
    Iris ware of, 31
    postcard of, 30
Ropevine, 60, 187
Rosa californica, 1, 164, 189
Rose, California Wild, 1, 164, 189
Rose-Bay, California, 86, 193
Round-Leaved Filaree, 127, 182
Rubus parviflorus, 165, 189
Rubus ursinus, 130, 189
Rumex salicifolius var. *salicifolius*, 120, 187

S

Sailor Caps, *39, 182*
Salazaria mexicana, 193, 198
Salix lasiolepis, 87, 187
Saltgrass, *40, 185*
Salvia apiana, 193, 198
Salvia carduacea, 193, 199
Salvia clevelandii, 193, 199
Salvia columbariae, 193, 199
Salvia dorrii var. *incana, 193, 199*
Salvia mellifera, 159, 193
Sambucus mexicana, 166, 195
San Diego Button Celery, *192, 193*
San Diego County
    as "hot spot" of biological diversity, 36
San Diego Sunflower, *123, 195*
Sandwort, California, *45, 111, 182*
Sarcodes sanguinea, 157, 193
Satureja douglasii, 52, 193
Saxifraga mertensiana, 111, 182
Scarlet Bugler, *193, 201*
Scoliopus bigelovii, 122, 187
Screw Bean, *128, 189*
Scripps, Ellen Browning, 9, 35, 40, 46
    commission of flora of California series, 36, 38, 75
    correspondence with Valentien, 39, 49, 50
    efforts to publish Valentien paintings, 51
    photograph of, 34
Sea Dahlia, *118, 195*
Sea Pink, *193, 196*
Sea Purslane, Western, *173, 187*
Seaside Daisy, *86, 195*
Sedge, *79, 185*
Sedum spathulifolium, 167, 189
Sequoia sempervirens, 168, 185
Sesuvium verrucosum, 173, 187
Shooting Star, *39, 69, 193*
Showy Penstemon, *195, 201*
Sidalcea diploscypha, 125, 182
Sidalcea malvaeflora ssp. *sparsifolia, 184, 190*
Silene hookeri, 54, 187
Silverback Fern, *53, 182*
Snow Plant, *157, 193*
Snow Queen, *38, 182*
Snowdrop Bush, *193, 196*
Solidago californica, 83, 195
Solon, Albert, 39, 46–48, 52

Sorghum halepense, 80, 185
Southern Mountain Misery, *176, 189*
Spartina foliosa, 124, 185
Splendid Mariposa Lily, *21, 185*
Splendid Triteleia, *173, 185*
Stinkweed, *174, 189*
Study of Yellow Roses, 76
Styrax officinalis var. *redivivus, 193, 196*
Sun Cup, *81, 190, 194*
Sword Fern, Western, *45, 182*
Sycamore, Western, *144, 189*
symbiosis, 134
Synthyris reniformis, 38, 182
Syntrichopappus fremontii, 46, 182

T

Tanbark Oak, *116, 187*
Teddy-Bear Cholla, *64, 190*
Tetracoccus dioicus, 48, 190
Thelypteris patens var. *patens, 122, 182*
Thimbleberry, *165, 189*
Thistle Sage, *193, 199*
Thistle, California, *58, 195*
Thurber's Buckwheat, *120, 187*
Thysanocarpus curvipes, 175, 189
Thysanocarpus radians, 175, 189
Tickseed, *61, 195*
Tidy Tips, *155, 195*
Toothwort, *25, 189*
Tornillo, *128, 189*
Torrey Pine, *134, 185*
Toxicodendron diversilobum, 40, 190
Toyon, *8, 96, 189*
Tree Clover, *136, 182*
Tree Tobacco, *136, 193*
Tree-Anemone, *26, 189*
Trichostema lanatum, 193, 198
Trifolium ciliolatum, 136, 182
Trifolium fucatum, 179, 189
Triphysaria eriantha ssp. *rosea, 46, 182*
Triteleia hendersonii var. *hendersonii, 173, 185*
Triteleia hyacinthina, 125, 182
Triteleia ixioides ssp. *splendens, 173, 185*
Triteleia peduncularis, 172, 185
Trout Lily, Western, *80, 182*

U

Utah Service Berry, *177, 189*

V

Valentien Pottery, 46–49, 75
Valentien, Albert Robert, 29–51, 75, 92
    approach to botanical illustration, 38, 40, 92
    career as decorator at Rookwood Pottery, 29–33
    education at University of Cincinnati School of Design, 29
    efforts to establish Valentien Pottery, 46–49
    flora of California series of, 38–46
    move to California, 36
    Pepper Tree, 34
    photographs of, 30, 31, 37, 44
    Study of Yellow Roses, 76
    travels in California, 39–41
Valentien, Anna Marie Bookprinter, 29, 33, 35, 75
    assistance with flora of California series, 40
    career as decorator at Rookwood Pottery, 31
    efforts to establish Valentien Pottery, 46, 47, 49
    photographs of, 31, 37, 44
Valley Oak, *151*, 187
Vanilla Leaf, *90*, 187
Velvet Cactus, *19*, 190
Vicia americana var. *americana*, *183*, 189
Victor's Gooseberry, *176*, 189
Viguiera laciniata, *123*, 195
Viola ocellata, *133*, 182

W

Wachtel, Elmer, 79, 82
Washington Lily, *103*, 187
Western Azalea, *152*, 193
Western Blue Flag, *98*, 187
Western Choke-Cherry, *177*, 189
Western Columbine, *87*, 187
Western Heart's Ease, *133*, 182
Western Poison Oak, *40*, 190
Western Sea Purslane, *173*, 187
Western Sword Fern, *45*, 182
Western Sycamore, *144*, 189
Western Trout Lily, *80*, 182
Western White Pine, *172*, 185
White Brodiaea, *125*, 182
White Fawn Lily, *79*, 187
White Hyacinth, *125*, 182
White Pine, Western, *172*, 185
White Sage, *193*, *198*
White, Edith, 82–83, 92
White-Flowered Bog Orchid, *123*, 187
White-Veined Wintergreen, *154*, 182
Wicker Buckwheat, *114*, 187
Wild Ginger, *16*, 187
Wild Hyacinth, *36*, 185
Wild Pea, *99*, *183*, 190
Wild Radish, *158*, 189
Willow Dock, *120*, 187
Witchgrass, *138*, 185
Wolf's Cholla, *65*, 190, *191*
Wood Strawberry, *131*, 182
Woodwardia fimbriata, *45*, 182
Woolly Bluecurls, *193*, *198*
Woolly Indian Paintbrush, *80*, 195
Wyethia angustifolia, *195*, *204*

X

Xerophyllum tenax, *169*, 185
Xylococcus bicolor, *170*, 193
Xylorhiza tortifolia var. *tortifolia*, *195*, *202*

Y

Yellow Skunk Cabbage, *105*, 185
Yerba Buena, *52*, 193
Yerba Mansa, *15*, 187
Yucca brevifolia, *129*, 187

Z

Zigadenus sp., *171*, 185